RADICAL SELF LOVE

By
Jeremy Witcher, Gayla Wick, Jessica Dugas,
Alison Verge, Pleasant Smith, Nancy White,
Crystal Cockerham, and Joanna Shakti

D1445779

TABLE OF CONTENTS

Introduction 5

1. Vision & Self-Love - *by Jeremy Witcher* 9

2. Limiting Beliefs – *by Gayla Wick* 23

3. Self-Sabotage - Silent Authenticity - *by Jessica Dugas* 37

4. Adaptation & Resilience – *by Alison Verge* 47

5. Implementing Boundaries – *by Pleasant Smith* 61

6. How to get Unstuck – *by Pleasant Smith* 69

7. Self- Love is Creating Goals - *by Nancy White* 79

8. Comfort Zone - Be a F.E.A.R. Rebel
   by Crystal Cockerham 89

9. 7 Shortcuts to Ecstatic Soulmate Attraction
   by Joanna Shakti 99

10. Rewriting the Definition of Self-Compassion
    by Jessica Dugas 113

11. Self-Love in Dating & Marriage - *by Gayla Wick* 123

INTRODUCTION
By Lori Ann Davis & Laura Menze

Self-love is a journey, not a destination. We will forever be on this journey growing and learning how to better love ourselves, especially in difficult, challenging times. Radical Self Love is about being conscious and fierce in your practices of self -love so that the challenging times become less challenging and you are open to giving and receiving Radical Love.

We all want to be part of satisfying loving relationships. This all starts with our relationship with ourselves, radically loving ourselves first. When you truly love yourself, you can then show up confident and secure enabling you to create strong, healthy, and loving relationships with others.

This book was designed to provide you with many different ideas and practices to help you along the way in your own Radical Self Love journey. You will learn how to love yourself before you can love others, learning how to create happiness within yourself instead of seeking it from others. When you are in charge of your happiness, no one can take that away from you. From this place of self-love, you can begin to attract the love you want and share that love in return. We will help you identify beliefs that might be holding you back so you can move beyond where you are to where you want to be. This often means trying new things and moving outside of your comfort zone to create the life and relationships you desire. Along the way, you will learn how to not only identify your boundaries but enforce them with love. All with the end goal of consciously loving yourself and sharing that love with others.

The beauty of this book, which is a compilation of chapters from 8 expert authors, is that each chapter includes practical tips you can implement right away. We are all here to support you on your journey toward Radical Self-Love. Enjoy reading this book and practicing the tips and techniques offered in each chapter. You might want to start by reading the book all the way through once and then going back to chapters that feel most pertinent to your current situation. Work through one chapter at a time as you feel called to do so. Our vision is that this book is one you will go back to often rereading chapters and working through them over and over again as you progress along your journey. We truly love you and want to support you.

Enjoy your journey!

~ Laura & Lori

About Lori Ann Davis

Lori is a Certified Relationship Specialist – Speaker- Author. She has a unique and passionate approach to love and relationships and believes that everyone deserves and can have the relationship of their dreams. Her mission is to provide you with the skills you need to have the unstoppable relationship you deserve.

She has a master's degree in clinical psychology with over 30 years' experience

empowering individuals and couples to live richer, happier lives. She provides relationship coaching to people throughout the world. Her practice spans the spectrum from dating and singles to working through divorce to renewing long-term marriages.

She is the author of *Unmasking Secrets to Unstoppable Relationships: How to Find, Keep and Renew Love and Passion in Your Life*, *365 Ways to Ignite Her Love*, *A Couples Love Journal*, and contributing author of *Ready, Set, Date*. She is also one of the coaches on the Radical Dating Documentary Show, www.Radical-dating.com

Information about all of Lori's coaching services, other products, blogs, and events can be found at www.lorianndavis.com.

About Laura Menze

Laura has a passion for helping to create more love in the world one person at a time. Although she has a Bachelor's degree in Communication and a Master's degree in Business Administration, she is most proud of her work as a Professional Certified Coach. She coaches clients in all areas of their lives, including career, and business, but specializes in Relationship Readiness Coaching for Singles. She is also a Matchmaker, teaches Professional Coaching to up and coming coaches, and is a contributing author to the book *Ready, Set, Date*.

Laura is so passionate about creating more love in the world one person at a time that she became the host of *The Denver Singles Summit* and was a featured coach on the docu-series, *Radical Dating – Breaking Through The Barriers to Find Lasting Love After 40*.

Finally, as an Ordained Minister, Laura marries her clients who've found love. She's a full service Love Professional eager to help those who are ready for a radical love. You can learn more about Laura and the variety of transformational professional services she offers at www.LauraMenze.com.

VISION AND SELF-LOVE
By Jeremy Witcher

*"If you have no vision of yourself in the future,
then you have nothing to live for."
– Les Brown*

Rachel was young and ambitious. Ever since she had seen
the local dance troupe perform at her mall, Rachel dreamed
one day she would be on stage. She imagined the thrill her
body would feel, moving to the music. Rachel practiced
bowing gracefully, reaching down to pick the inevitable
rose tossed by an adoring fan. At age eight, Rachel knew
what she wanted. The plan was made. All she had to do was
follow it.

Fast forward 20 years and Rachel stands at a window in her
apartment - the AC unit on the fritz. She clears the sweat
from her forehead. In the background, bickering children,
the occasional slammed door, and a barking dog collide. "It's
not fair!" she hears her daughter yell to her son, who was
enacting some sibling torture.

It was not fair! Nothing leading to this moment seemed
remotely fair. Rachel gazed out the food-speckled window,
wondering how she had gotten there and why these
windows were so dirty. She forgot the plate in her hand until

it splashed into the sink. Rachel felt her wet T-shirt. How had things gone so wrong?

Ah, Rachel. Her story is one told millions of times around the world in every language and every culture. She is our sister, our neighbor, our wife, our daughter, our Self. Change the place, the smells, the dialog, or the gender. Put in any details you want, and we all have been Rachel.

We all remember having dreams, and yet they disappear. How does this happen?

Vision, purpose, drive, goals, and mission are words seldom used in the same sentence with Self-love. Indeed, these words seem to be the opposite of loving one's Self. But in this chapter, we explore why and how Self-love is the key to fulfilling your life vision and living a life full of purpose and love.

There isn't a counselor, guru, priest, or therapist who doesn't repeatedly encounter the client who says they are "lost". When asked what they want to do with their life, the usual answer is, "I don't know." Dig a little deeper and what is really meant by, "I don't know." is "I am tired of trying to figure this out." or "I know the answer but don't like it." We all know what we want, and we all have a vision for our life, even if we feel like we can't remember that vision.

So, how does anyone forget their vision in the first place? And more importantly, what does this have to do with Self-love?

The easy answer is that somewhere along the way, people choose paths that serve the wants and needs of others versus the wants and needs of themselves. In other words, societal pressures and norms have won the day at the expense of the individual Self.

Now, before we go down the rabbit hole that is bashing society, let's remember why we have community, culture, structure, and rules. But, before we talk about why we need these things, let's talk about what happens when we don't have them.

Anyone who has ever traveled for an extended period or moved to a new culture knows something about culture shock. Culture shock is the disorientation encountered by someone who is abruptly subjected to an unknown culture, way of life, or established beliefs. Manifestations of culture shock may include all or some of the following; anger, boredom, food and weight issues, homesickness, exhaustion, withdrawal, hostility, impulsiveness, mood swings, and suicidal thoughts or actions.

So, obviously the culture we are in plays a significant role in how we function in the world, or it wouldn't be such a big deal when we move from culture to culture. We would adapt without adverse side effects. But, without our distinct and learned culture, our bodies and minds shut down. Why is this? To answer this question, we need to understand the purpose these cultures serve.

The whole intent of culture is to standardize, normalize, and mobilize individuals into a force more substantial than the individual itself. Societies provide ease of access and shared understandings. These societal understandings may be as simple as knowing which side of the street to drive on, or they may be more subtle and nuanced. But each rule (spoken or unspoken) plays an essential role in how we maneuver through our lives. The purpose of civilization is to standardize the experience for future growth.

Think of going into a grocery store and not having anything labeled. Worse yet, imagine that there were no rules as to where the items in the store were placed. One day the milk might be front and center of the store. The next day it might be shoved to a corner. Cereal may be by the pet food or near the cheese, depending on the mood of the employee stocking the shelves. Think about what it would be like to shop in that environment. There are no labels, no definitions, no instructions, no order, and no understanding. Some of you are having a panic attack just thinking about it. You could say that this store was lacking a culture. Or, I guess you could say the cultural norm (if any) was confusion. That isn't a great foundation to build trust and commitment with your customers. I know I wouldn't want to shop there.

Now think of your favorite organized store and imagine finding your weekly shopping items nicely labeled in their designated aisles. Knowing just a bit about the environment or the culture of the store allows you to plan and function within that system appropriately and efficiently. Knowing this information will enable you to set your expectations and adjust accordingly. Not convinced that cultural and societal norms are needed? Let me use another example - your body.

Think of all the things your body does every day without you thinking about it. It functions seamlessly based on a set of instructions given it. You don't think about your body until something goes wrong. You expect everything to work and work well. You don't want to spend time telling your heart to beat every second or remind your lungs that they need to expand when breathing. You wish your blood to flow, your limbs to work, and your skin to heal when scratched or burned. You want the body to work consistently and efficiently. Why? Because you have other tasks on which you want to focus. You have other desires you wish to fulfill. You have other things to create. Having systems in place that run your body without you thinking about it allows you to use the rest of your resources for becoming who you want to be.

With or without our knowing it, we are making decisions based on what keeps us safely within the margin of normality inside any given society. Every interaction builds upon the last until a community given identity carves a place for us. The good part of this programmed or labeled version of ourselves is that we have a place within the group. We have a name or structure that tells us how we fit in and function within the collective and what the expectations of that collective are. And this understanding allows others to interact cohesively with us. We then feel accepted, and this helps build confidence and wellbeing. From this identity, we choose from a predetermined selection of what is best for us, keeping life simple, safe, and productive.

In other words, if we were a grocery item, we would be found quickly and used appropriately. Or if we were an organ of the body, we would know when and how to help the body function as a whole. Society has helped us find our purpose and vision.

Our communal label (or identity) is only a problem when we want to change the label, and there is no clear cultural path to do so. Remember, the job of our culture is to keep the norm. If what you envision for yourself is not recognized by your culture, this is going to be a problem. Any movement by you, away from the typical pattern of your culture, will naturally be fraught with resistance. So basically, if we want to change and grow (which every human does), our culture will fight hard against us.

Let's go back to Rachel. Why didn't she become that dancer she wanted to be? Most likely, the identity Rachel envisioned for herself pushed the limits of her society. Dancing wasn't within the margin of normalcy. Maybe she came from a community of farmers who didn't value dance as a profession. Therefore, there was nothing within the structure she lived in that supported her vision. Over time, Rachel's vision was challenged and questioned, and Rachel eventually caved to the collective societal forces around her. But don't be hard on her. And don't be hard on her society. Her society didn't mean to crush her dreams. The opposite is true. Her culture wanted to keep her safe and itself stable.

Now, what if Rachel grew up in a performance culture. Her mother was a ballerina, and her father was a famous stage director. Then the norm of her community would have allowed her to pursue her dream. Only if she departed from her cultural norm (let's say to become a farmer) would Rachel meet resistance. So, it doesn't matter the subject, dream, or vision we chose. If it doesn't fit with the norm of a group, it will be challenging to find support.

Now you understand why we have all been Rachel. There are always (in every society) individuals meant to keep the standards, people who play on the fringes, and the "Rachels" who expand or change its borders. The fact is, each of us moves in and out of the roles of society. Sometimes we are society's standard. Occasionally, we are playing on the edges of what is acceptable. And other times, we are way outside the boundaries. We vary in our societal position as we move through different stages of our life, and from topic to topic.

So, what does this have to do with loving ourselves? Everything! Each human needs a community to thrive. Even those individuals who seem separate to themselves inevitably find community, be it sometimes of the nonhuman species. It is from our community that we learn how we want to mold and shift our expansion. When a community rejects an individual, it sends a strong signal back to the individual that it is not wanted and unloved. Receiving this signal once or twice may not be destructive. It can work to curb the careless behavior of the individual. But to repeatedly be bombarded with the message from your community that your decisions are unwanted starts a dangerous chain reaction for an individual. Unwanted equals unloved. Quite commonly, the individual turns inward, embracing the message of the collective and begins to self-sabotage. They learn to dislike themselves. For most, the resistance of the community to one's dreams is more than they know how to handle. And at the end of the day, many give up and walk away. They often hold resentment to their society for crushing their dreams and dislike for themselves because they allowed their community to dictate their life.

So, what is the solution? Well, if you have a vision, and that vision does not fit within your current cultural norm, you must find a new community. You must find a new culture. But this is NOT easy because you will go through culture shock, and I want to talk about Self-love within the framework of culture shock because each vision is, at its core, asking us to change the status quo of our current culture. Pick a topic, pick a place, pick anything you want. Every goal, vision, dream, asks if we are willing to take a path away from the current situation we know. And inevitably, the decision to follow such a path will shock our system. So, let's talk about culture shock.

Culture shock has four stages:

1. The Honeymoon Stage
2. The Negotiation Stage
3. The Adjustment Stage
4. The Adaptation Stage

The Honeymoon Stage

Here the individual is enthralled with the idea of the unusual. It is inspiring and exciting. There is little to no real understanding of the culture. Everything about this new environment is "wonderful." Here is where we find Rachel as an eight-year-old dreaming of becoming a dancer.

The Negotiation Stage

Then the person faces some resistance as they move around in their new environment. They start to realize that not everything would be as smooth as they thought. The standards and norms of this particular system are different from what they are used to, and they don't feel like they fit in. There is a war between old and new cultures. However, there is still some lingering euphoria from the Honeymoon Stage, so the individual dismisses these difficulties and negotiates with themselves, saying, "It isn't that bad." or "These problems are an anomaly."

The individual must choose what they will lose. The consequences of this loss can be overwhelming. Here is where significant mind and body stress can develop and, if not addressed, can become chronic. The individual must choose a path that makes them genuinely happy. For Rachel, this is where she started to give in. Maybe she told herself she would put off her dream of dancing for a little while until she conformed.

And here is where I want to pause. This stage right here is where the very idea of Self-love gets attacked. Why?

Because up till now, everything has been because of Self-love. The love of one's Self propels the sense of a new identity, project, vision, or existence; all these things. Up until now, the sky has been the limit. The individual has pursued what will be most fulfilling and what gives them the most passion. But now that they have hit the negotiation stage of their new environment, the question remains. Are they going to choose the love for themselves, or are they going to choose the love of their community?

Adjustment Stage

To move onto the Adjustment Stage, the person must accept the truth about their surroundings. They must realize that their dreams and visions are never going to have the support they need from their current culture. They must seek assistance elsewhere. They start looking for others who might be on the fringe of their existing community, or they find a different one altogether. This stage is awkward as it requires the individual to be in two worlds at the same time. They typically hide the developing side of themselves from their old community to protect themselves. They will inevitably feel anger and hurt for the difficult choices they must make.

Adaptation Stage

Here the person finds themselves adjusting and adapting to their new society and finding an identity within that new community. They have come to some understanding and peace regarding their old culture. The individual has received positive reinforcement from their new surroundings, letting them know their dreams and visions are wanted and loved. The support from this new community builds the individual's confidence to keep pursuing their vision, and in doing so, they find themselves more and more in love with whom they are becoming. The once hard decisions are now worth making because of the success and inward Self-love they have.

Many of you reading this chapter have come into this world to shift the norms. You have read these words and can identify with the feelings. I want to encourage you that one, you are not alone, and two, you have what it takes. The irony is that the societies that have given you such a hard time will, in time, start to change as more and more individuals pursue differing paths. Whenever you have a new idea or vision, use these simple steps to help navigate your decisions.

1. What part of my idea will my community support or not support?
2. How big is this vision? Is it a small vision or a life vision?
3. How committed am I to this vision? Is it worth the change?
4. If I don't choose this, will I blame my community or myself?
5. If I do choose this, what joy and love will it bring me?
6. Where do I need to find guidance and support to achieve this change?

7. What and when do I share with my old community if ever? Am I prepared to deal with the consequences either way?

Asking these few questions will help set your expectations before you start. It will also clarify why it is you may not have achieved a former vision.

Remember, not every thought is a life dream. But, there are those ideas that your soul tells you are your destiny. These make up your life vision, and you must listen to those ideas. Each change requires a gain and a loss. But the changes that bring you closer to who you are will also bring you closer to loving yourself. The two are inseparable. So, if you find that you are unhappy with yourself, you have made a choice you didn't like. The good news is, you don't have to keep making that choice. With understanding and a supportive community, you can craft a life that is in line with your vision and an experience that you ultimately love. Self-love is never something you should sacrifice.

I trust these few words point you in the right direction and give you the courage to dream again. You are the answer to a question the world has asked. There is a place for you and all your dreams, but only as you love yourself.

About Jeremy Witcher

Jeremy Witcher is a Seer, celebrated Media Producer, Best-Selling Author, Spiritual Mentor, and Teacher. He has been a student of Prophet Calvin since they met in 2004 and currently works as a Teaching Facilitator and Director of Public Affairs for Neumology®. Together, with Prophet Calvin Witcher, they oversee the Neumology® community where they teach their students practical revelatory truth. He is also a husband to Prophet Calvin and father of their four sons. You can learn more about Jeremy at:

https://neumology.com

LIMITING BELIEFS

By Gayla Wick

"If you accept a limiting belief,
then it will become a truth for you."
— Louise Hay

Ancient mariners believed the earth was flat - limiting their travels for fear of sailing off the edge into an unknown abyss. For millennia human flight and space travel were thought impossible. Skyscrapers, cell phones, Wi-Fi and countless other innovations were once thought to be pure fantasy. To be human is to have self-imposed limits on what's possible, that is until we don't. Someone or some experience or dream must seize our imagination in ways that cause us to shed old ideas for new.

As a small child I thought lunch always came before dessert until the day my grandmother came to visit. Off we went to the Dairy Queen for ice cream. This was strange as I did not recall eating lunch. My young mind was in awe as our hot fudge sundaes were followed with burgers and fries. What a day that was! This experience was the beginning of a new way of thinking for me.

Limiting beliefs are just that – beliefs that limit our experiences, our ability to move forward in the direction of our dreams. I see this every time I meet people who've given up on love. When we talk about why they are still single when they really desire a love relationship, the limiting beliefs come spilling out.

We all have them – those pesky thoughts, opinions and beliefs that keep us stuck right where we are. This is more than annoying – its life limiting in ways that kill our dreams. Our individual limiting beliefs seem riveted to us regardless of how much we want to think otherwise. They are real, they are insidious, and they are dream killers.

When I thought about writing a book, my limiting beliefs decided to show up with a ferocity that knocked me back. Who was I to write a book? I thought the only successful authors were people who had been on a writing, journalism or English literature path for years. I let these life limiting beliefs inhibit me until I discovered that I had a choice. I could let them sabotage my deepest desires to write a life altering book to help singles find love or I could change my mindset.

Ah, easily said, but not so easily done. You probably know what I'm talking about. You may have heard about limiting beliefs from self-help authors and speakers or read something about them. Seems like a popular topic of conversation, yet, most of us still have way too many beliefs that aren't easily going away. What's really happening?

In my experience, it's common to think simple awareness is enough to magically make limiting beliefs vanish or at least render them ineffectual. I wish it was that easy for both myself and for you. Becoming aware of personal beliefs that do not serve our best interests or highest goals is only the first step in a process. In this chapter I'm going to share with you a five-step guide that will awaken your desire and ability to shift your personal limiting beliefs about love, dating, marriage and relationships.

This is a subtle yet powerful method for taking limiting beliefs that have not been helpful to your personal growth and nudging them out of your present reality. Our minds can be like a courtroom. When we tell ourselves something, we then collect evidence to support our beliefs. This can be especially damaging for singles who've been searching for love for what seems like an eternity without results and perhaps even a great amount of pain and heartbreak. This is why it's critically important to shift your mindset beginning right now.

Not having the love relationship you've imagined and dreamed of for so long might be where your limiting beliefs are anchored. The good news is that you have the power to take action to change your love and dating results. The challenging news is you have to change your mindset to have a new, profoundly more positive experience. If this is where you are, you may have just sighed, or perhaps felt that sinking feeling in your gut, but stick with me. What I'm about to share with you is simple, but it takes effort on your part. You can do it and you can use this process on any limiting belief.

I encourage you to make a critical decision right now. Be

open to what I'm about to share with you and save any judgements for later. You don't have to believe anything, just don't busy your mind with doubt. As you go through the next five steps do so with a relaxed and open mind to the real possibility that these subtle shifts will begin the powerful process of releasing your personal limiting beliefs in favor of a deep knowing that you can change your results.

Limiting Beliefs Change Exercise

STEP 1: You'll need a pen and notebook or paper. I recommend you write instead of type because I want you to feel the mind-body connection for best results. Note: Studies have shown that handwriting activates different areas of the brain allowing us to slow down and better understand, assimilate and remember information.

Find a comfortable place to sit. Have a warm drink by your side.

Take a few minutes to center yourself by taking several deep breaths and relax into your body. This is a good time to hold your warm cup of tea or coffee, savor the aroma and feel the warmth of the cup in your hands. Put it down and close your eyes.

Think about why you are still single. Answer these 3 questions:

- What do I tell my family about being single?
- What do I tell my friends?
- What do I tell myself?

Begin writing your answers. A paragraph for each should be good. Be totally honest. In order to shift beliefs, you must come to terms with what they are. Only you know what's truly in your heart. Write down everything that shows up. This is no time for judgements! I know this may be a bit uncomfortable but know in your heart that you can do this, and your efforts now will bring extraordinary results later as you proceed through the rest of this exercise. Here's an example:

My parents keep asking me why I don't have a boyfriend or husband. I tell them my job is too important and I don't have time for relationships or dating. I'm too picky and besides all the good ones are taken or gay. I tell other family members that I'm dating, but the right one just hasn't come along.

I tell my friends that men are just too much trouble. They have too much baggage and I'm afraid of losing who I am if I get in a serious relationship. I'm perfectly fine being single. That's the way I like it. No one around to tell me what to do or how to spend my time or money.

When alone, I feel like I'm really missing out and know I want someone to love and adore me. I am so jealous of my friend's relationships. I have lots of love to give, but I'm afraid of making a mistake. My last relationship was a disaster. I attract all the wrong types of men. A man just wants sex anyway. He'll probably cheat on me. I'm afraid of getting my heart broken.

This is just an example. Spend as much time as you need to get all your thoughts on paper.

Take a break. Congratulate yourself on completing this important first step.

When you are ready get a highlighter or pen and go back to your paragraphs and underline each limiting belief. You may be surprised to find out how many negative things you believe about men/women, love, dating and marriage.

STEP 2: Take out a new sheet of paper. Write *Limiting Beliefs* at the top.

Write each belief that you highlighted or underlined – each one on a separate line. Don't leave anything out. Here's an example.

- I don't have time for a love relationship
- I'm too picky
- All the good ones are taken or gay
- Men are too much trouble
- Men bring too much baggage to a relationship
- I'll lose myself if I get in a love relationship
- I'm happy being single
- Men are controlling
- I don't trust myself to choose a partner
- I only attract the wrong types of men
- All men want is sex
- He will probably cheat on me
- I'll get my heart broken

Now that you have your list take more time to reflect on your deepest beliefs about love, dating and marriage. Add anything else that comes to you. In order to get the most from this exercise you'll want to make your list as complete as possible before moving to the next step.

STEP 3: Take out a new sheet of paper. Notice that your previous list of limiting beliefs is most likely written in the present tense. That's because these beliefs are currently active in your conscious and subconscious. Now we're going to gently begin the shifting process - one step at a time.

Take each belief and change the verbs from present to past tense. Here's an example:

- I didn't think I had time for a love relationship
- I thought I was too picky
- I used to think all the good guys were taken or gay
- I thought men were too much trouble
- In the past I thought men brought too much baggage to a relationship
- I felt I would lose myself if I fell in love
- I was happy being single
- Men were always too controlling
- I didn't trust myself to choose a partner
- In the past I only attracted the wrong types of men
- I believed all men just wanted sex
- I knew he would probably cheat on me
- I was afraid my heart would be broken

Take time to complete this step using the past tense verbs and words that resonate best with you. Remember this is just an example. Your personal story is incredibly unique, and your thoughts are yours to shift in this exercise. We are about halfway through this process so now may be a good time to take a break for a day or two while you reflect on the work you've done so far. Add any limiting beliefs that may pop up during the next few days or weeks. Be sure to document and re-word them from present to past tense.

Although this part of the exercise may seem simple, it's a powerful stimulus to your mind that these ideas belong in the past. This creates space for you to have new, more empowering beliefs in your present.

STEP 4: Take out a new sheet of paper. Write **My New Beliefs** at the top. Take each past tense belief and pivot it from a limiting belief (negative) to a more life affirming (positive) one. Here's an example:

- I have plenty of time for a love relationship
- I am discerning and open for love
- There are many great available men for me to date
- The man I choose to be with is healthy and emotionally mature
- My special someone has a successful life
- The man of my dreams respects and values who I am and loves me for me
- I deeply desire an authentic love connection
- I always stand up for myself and make good choices
- I fully trust myself to choose a partner
- I attract the perfect partner for me

- I believe sex is an important part of a loving intimate relationship
- The man in my life is loyal and dedicated to only me
- My heart is open to love and being loved

This part of the exercise serves as the backbone of your new life story. Be sure to use only words and positive thoughts that work best for you. Take plenty of time to complete this step. Sit with what you've written and reflect on how this new dialog feels. You don't need to believe any of these new ideas yet. Review your new list every day for the next two weeks. Then move to the next step when you are ready.

STEP 5: Time for more paper. In this last step you will be writing your **New Story**. Using some or all of the items on your list write a new story for your future - as if it is happening now. Don't be concerned if you have doubts about whether it is possible. Take your time and allow yourself to visualize what you desire in your love relationship experience.

Write about your new partner and how you will love and support each other. Imagine how you are feeling in this new relationship. See the future as you've dreamed about and allow the possibility to exist without stressing about anything. Believe it is so and if that seems too difficult, just practice being open to the possibilities. Let your doubts fall gently away.

Once you have written your new story it's important to read it every day. Read it to yourself with joy and enthusiasm even on days you may be struggling with doubt. Read it out

warm people. I know this isn't always how we feel, but it's so important for you to spend most of your time with a positive open mind. It's okay to relax and have fun with your new story. Laugh at yourself occasionally, especially as you tell your new story. A client shared she read her new story to her cat and he was thoroughly unimpressed. We both laughed and she continued to delight in telling him about her new love life anyway.

Addressing our personal limiting beliefs is a process. This process happens gradually as we take baby steps to release our mind's hold on what we once believed. Our thoughts, beliefs and ideas were developed one step at a time, so please be patient with yourself as you go forward. Limiting beliefs really can shift into supportive, empowering beliefs that bring our dreams into reality.

"The limits of your beliefs are only limited by your beliefs."
— Anonymous Zen Master

About Gayla Wick

Gayla Wick, Denver Love Coach, author, and speaker is the creator of the highly acclaimed "It's All About You" Love Coaching Program for single women. Once a true love skeptic, Gayla shows those who've been disappointed in love how to move past pain and struggle to attract an authentic love relationship. She's the author of The Art of Attracting Authentic Love (A transformational Four-Step Process). Information about her coaching services, book, videos and blog can be found at www.GaylaWick.com.

SELF-SABOTAGE: SILENT AUTHENTICITY

By Jessica S. Dugas

"Be honest.
Speak your truth.
Don't be afraid to do either."
— Unknown

I've never really thought of myself as someone who is afraid to speak. I'll typically tell people how it is with a little attitude - that's the New England in me! I'll tell almost anyone about my day and the things I love like music, movies, games, meditation, essential oils, my family, plant-based living, Patriots football, and more. To those I know well, I allow myself to express how I feel on more hot topics such as politics, religion, parenting, and sex.

What I've realized about myself, is that what I'm not afraid of, is talking. I AM, however, often afraid to speak.

Speaking Authentically

Being afraid to speak authentically, to speak the truth of who you really are is a learned behavior. It comes from things like our life experiences, our demographics (age, sex, education, geographic location, ethnicity, religion & spirituality), how we're raised, personal morals, and more.

It's not placing blame or playing the victim. For example, saying, "This happened to me growing up, so because of that I have fears." It's simply the circumstances of your life, how they were interpreted, and the choices that were made in response to them.

There are a lot of ways and reasons that we can learn this behavior I'm calling Silent Authenticity. It's very similar to how we define stress, there are good stressors and bad stressors in our lives, but in the end it's still stress. If there's too much of it, it can have negative effects on our whole being, body, mind, and spirit. It's the same thing with silent authenticity. There's good silence such as someone saying, "Shh, don't spoil your sister's birthday surprise!" or "Don't tell anyone yet because it's early, but we're having another baby!". There's also harmful silence such as, "Don't tell anyone I just did that to you or I'll hurt you again." or "Don't talk about that, that's dumb." Altogether, regardless of intention, it's still silence. It's in this silence that we can learn to hide who we truly are.

Unfortunately, even though every single person I know on this planet has gone through silencing experiences, almost all of us continue the pattern in silencing others through the words that we use. We do this through constant criticism. Even never-ending complaining about our own situations helps silence others in that they begin to feel their own experiences are insignificant and don't deserve to be heard.

Consequences of Silence

What happens as a result of this silence? The result of

what can happen is why I have become so passionate about learning to be authentic. It can go far beyond simply self-sabotage. As I have been on my journey of growing, changing, and becoming a better person, I had developed an even more, at times paralyzing fear of being my authentic self. I became afraid that people weren't going to understand me or that they weren't going to like me just for sharing my thoughts. Even in my mindset work of visualizing being my full, authentic self I was seeing myself being physically harmed by other people during that process.

Not being yourself means not allowing anyone else to see the real you. It becomes easy to attract the wrong people into your life. You repel the right people including ideal clients that are going to help grow your business. You repel the right people who could become the best friends you've ever had because they love you for you or the ideal partner you have been longing for.

In my case, I was missing out on opportunities because I was riding this bus of fear. It wasn't until I realized that this silent authenticity was manifesting itself in a physical way, that I understood the negative power it can have over our whole being. See, in this process of feeling like I couldn't speak or live in my authenticity, which is all centered around that throat chakra, I began developing blocks and infections in that entire area of my body. My teeth, jaw, tongue, throat, and neck all became incredibly inflamed. It has literally taken every single tool in my self-care arsenal, as well as help from others, and fierce determination to move past these toxic thoughts and fears to allow myself to live.

3 Steps to Overcoming Silent Authenticity

So, what can you do? What can you do when you recognize that you are living in silent authenticity? Here are three key points to begin recognizing this pattern in yourself so you can move past it.

1. ***Understanding***. We need to recognize that like everything else in our lives, we have zero control over anyone else but ourselves. It is in that awareness that we can move forward with the following changes.

2. ***You are in control***. With this understanding comes a profound awakening where we realize that we are in control of our own authenticity and living our own truth. There are NO circumstances of our lives or other people's thoughts and opinions of us that can control us if we don't allow them to. This one can be a hard pill to swallow as it is so much easier to blame someone else, or some specific event or circumstance for our problems. Because then, we're not wrong, right? No one wants to admit that they actually had control the whole time and didn't know it or didn't take advantage of it. So, while it may be hard, it gives us an awareness that allows us to begin making changes to move forward.

3. ***Just do it***. Now that you understand that you can't control anyone else, and you own the fact that living authentically is completely on you, you have a divine responsibility, and honor, to do just that. Following through with this step, not only living authentically

but SPEAKING your truth loud and clear, is probably the most important thing you will ever do in your lifetime because now you're creating a space for other people to do the same.

Creating a Safe Space

This might be enough information for you and that's ok! However, I know that many of you reading this book have a deep desire to change the world and I want you to know that this work you're doing, fully loving yourself, IS changing the world! With this desire to help others while working on our own self-love, we can now be intentional about creating that safe space!

Have you ever had someone express thanks to you because your actions or words paved the way for them? That's what happens when we begin to show up authentically and speak with our authentic voices, even if it isn't expressed to us. It's amazing when that happens organically but what would it look like if we could create this space intentionally? Here are some specific things we can do to help ourselves, and others, feel safe in getting out of silent authenticity.

To create this space, we need to be mindful of the words we tell ourselves. Our truth deserves to be heard and respected.

To create this space, we need to be mindful of our words to others and know that we all, at one time or another, have been silenced. Their truths deserve to be heard and respected.

To create this space, we need to honor each other's truths when they're different from our own. Practice meditating from your crown chakra, from a neutral place of unconditional love and respect. If it's your practice to pray, pray for the ability to love unconditionally, with joy and ease. If you have a hard time with either of these things, simply getting in the practice of responding to differing truths with something like, "I honor your truth," and making the choice to move on without feeling the need to argue or defend your own truth, is truly an amazing exercise.

To create this space, we need to release any expectations that we are going to receive the same level of unconditional love and respect that we give. In those moments that we feel unaccepted for who we are, and we start to feel small and silenced again, release those expectations. Just love them more deeply and more fully with your whole being.

To create this space, we need to go forth in our truths knowing that there will be times when I, when you, and when everyone else is going to fall short of both living in and creating a space of authenticity. When you fall short, which you will, know that you're safe, and loved, and not alone.

Today, stand in your truth and introduce yourself to the world all over again. Trust me when I tell you that if you've been living in silent authenticity most of your life like I have, then I know you've done a really good job of being who everyone else has wanted you to be. Take some deep breaths and get ready to express the TRUE you, not who or what you think others want to hear from you.

So, let's get up and do this in whatever way feels best to you! There's no wrong way, only what feels the most in alignment with where you are right now! Here are some suggestions for you:

- Go live on social media
- Write a blog
- Write in your journal
- Send an email or letter to a loved one
- Call your best friend
- Stand in front of the mirror

In your authentic reintroduction to the world, don't hold back! Talk specifics first.

- What's your name? - I shared my name and a little story behind it.
- How old are you? - This helps you mark time for when you do this exercise in the future.
- Who do you love? - Who are you to the most important people in your life?
- Where do you live, currently? - Geographics are an important part of who you are.
- What does spirituality look like to you? - Do you have faith or a specific spiritual practice that is important to your life?
- What do you do for work or how do you spend your day? – When I do this, I share about my business

and what my business stands for as I realize it is an extension of myself and my personal ideals!

- What things do you love? – Are you into music, movies, your family?
- What do you consider to be your flaws? - Be honest with this but do NOT tear yourself down!

Go back to the section about creating space for authenticity if you need some gentle reminders here! For example, I shared in my statement about the fact that I'm easily distracted but I also shared that it has helped to shape who I am in that I've had to teach myself how to be more organized and prepared!

What little quirks about you make you, you? - This is a space for you to open up and be silly! For example, I randomly burst out in song! HA! You say a word, it reminds me of a song, and next thing you know I'm singing it! Sometimes, those songs exist, sometimes I make them up, and sometimes I even write my own rap parodies to popular songs. - Express yourself... the TRUE you!

Here's the amazing thing: This is going to change over time. I wrote out my first reintroduction to the world 4 years ago and it has been a beautiful thing to look back on to realize that while little things have changed, my heart, and who I am at my core, truly hasn't. I am still beautiful, authentic me, but I'm no longer silent!

My hope is that in doing this exercise, it will give you the space to be your authentic self. If there is any part of you that you feel you can't share with the world, reach out to someone you trust and allow them to hold your hand and support you in the process.

About Jessica Dugas

Jessica Dugas is an Intuitive Mentor, International Best-Selling Author, and Inspirational Entertainer. She's the creator and host of The Breakthrough Show and the Project Joy Podcast!

She's passionate about helping women empower themselves to live with less stress and more joy, bringing her coaching skills, healing modalities, authentic intuition, holistic lifestyle choices, and spirituality to her Illuminate Your Spirit Community. Outside of her business, Jessica is a wife and homeschooling mom of 6 beautiful children, living a vegan lifestyle. You can find out more about Jessica here: https://www.jessicadugas.com

ADAPTATION & RESILIENCE
by Alison Verge

"Do not judge me by my success, judge me by how many times I fell down and got back up again."
– Nelson Mandela

Oh, So Naive!

I must not cry…. I need to be strong. I can't let other people see how weak I am. If I ignore the problem, it will all just go away, right? I'll just do everything the way it's always been done then life will be safe and nothing horrible will happen.

These are all subconscious thoughts I had during tough times and you may have as well. I thought it was admirable to never show signs of weakness. It took many years and some very rough situations for me to finally realize that resilience is not about smiling, pretending everything is OK and acting fearless. This is the great fallacy about what it means to be resilient. In fact, this misperception leads to the opposite, driving people towards unhealthy choices in their lives strictly out of fear. The fear of facing adversity and change.

The greatest transformation happened in my life when I

embraced the changes that were occurring and discovered how to deal with hurdles along the way.

Seriously Universe? WTF?

Things were great! My kids and business were thriving, my husband still loved me, I was in the best shape of my life and I was finally getting some time to really focus on my own needs and wants! Of course, I had problems like many of you and if you asked me prior to that time, I probably would have said that my life was difficult at times. But I had no idea till much later how much tougher things would become and how hard I would have to fight to feel joy again.

Five years ago, a skiing accident resulted in a condition called Complex Regional Pain Syndrome (CRPS) also nicknamed "the suicide disease" or "the invisible illness" as the symptoms are not always visibly obvious. It often goes undiagnosed and the pain level is higher than childbirth or amputation without drugs (McGill pain index scale). There did not appear to be a lot of hope beyond prescription opiates that I did not want to take. Being a former exercise fanatic now wheelchair bound outside the home, this was pure torture – both physically and emotionally!

Unfortunately, around the same time, just after planning a large renovation to our home, my marriage of 20 years ended. It felt like the universe had it in for me. After a lot of pondering, I knew I had two choices: to fight back or throw in the towel and give in to the pain and sorrow. I could very easily just take the drugs to dull my senses. But with two daughters, a successful career, and a healthy body I had worked my whole life for, I was not prepared to accept this fate. My future was going to be bright, one way or another.

I researched and tried countless therapies. My limits were tested. There were times the pain was so horrible it made me sick to my stomach, but I kept the finish line in site. Little did I know that through this journey, not only would I go into remission which is very rare, but I would also come out stronger than I ever thought possible. I had a new level of resilience that I am sure will benefit me for years to come.

What Exactly is Resilience?

The dictionary defines resilience as *tending to recover from or adjust easily to misfortune or change.* Does this mean that people who are resilient don't experience suffering? Absolutely not. In fact, becoming resilient requires emotional distress in order to learn the best practices for dealing with them and learning to buffer the adverse effects. Resilience is not a character trait you are born with. Anyone can learn to develop the necessary thoughts, behaviors, and actions to build it up. Each person's level of resilience varies.

Take for example two patients suffering a lot of pain from the same injury being asked to rate it on a scale of 1-10. Patient #1 may rate it a 10/10 as the worst pain imaginable. Patient #2 may rate it a 5/10 being tolerable to them.

Everyone copes differently with life's struggles, what affects one person may have little impact on another. Similarly, people can demonstrate high resilience in one area of their lives, in their workplace, but be less resilient in another, in their personal life. A doctor may be able to calmly deal with his or her patients but explode with anger when faced with conflict at home.

How Does One Become Resilient?

There is no quick fix. Many strategies are easy on their own, but resilience comes with practice over time and has been shown to be more prevalent in individuals who use a variety of coping strategies. I know I would not be sitting here right now with a smile on my face, having just completed a good workout without adopting these key practices:

Health and Wellness - An unhealthy mind and/or body will make any struggle twice as hard. Think of it like a soldier putting on his armor preparing for war. Being healthy is the best armor we have to fight life's battles.

Exercise – There are many excuses why we can't find the time to exercise but If there is a will, there really is a way. With your doctor's approval, try and exercise at least 3 times per week. There are plenty of quick YouTube workout routines you can find to do at home or incorporate into your daily ritual. Get creative and climb your office or condo stairs, do water aerobics, a Wii dance video etc. I find the best time to work out is the morning, so nothing interferes. It also provides an energy boost, which is an extra bonus if going through a rough time.

Sleep –Try to get at least 7 hours a night. Every problem seems so much worse without adequate rest. Write down any to-dos for the next day so they do not weigh on your mind. Keep a notepad handy by your bed in case you wake up with a pressing thought preventing you from going back to sleep. Write it down and let it go!

Eat well – Our system goes out of alignment causing our moods to go downhill when we make bad choices like: skipping meals - especially breakfast which leads to low blood sugar, likely making you feel sluggish and tired. Also cutting out entire food groups will make it difficult to get all the essential nutrients you need leading to mood swings and decreased energy. Some of my favorite foods that I eat every day to boost moods are dark chocolate, berries, raw nuts and avocado.

Eating too many unhealthy carbohydrates that are processed, such as white bread and pastries, trigger a fast rise and fall in blood sugars. This can lead to low energy and irritability.

Of course, it is ok to treat yourself, but limit these to once or twice per week or choose better options like dark chocolate. Ensure the easy to grab snack options are healthy options. Eat home cooked meals as much as possible. No time? There are so many available quick and healthy recipes that can be prepared in as little as 15 minutes or less.

Therapy – Sometimes we need extra support beyond what we can do for ourselves. Know the signs. If it ever starts to become too much, seek out help. This does not make you weak, it takes courage to ask for help and it is always a good idea to talk things out even if the situation is not in crisis.

Therapy comes in all forms these days - coaching, psychotherapy, psychiatry, social work etc. In my opinion, trust and comfort between the client and therapist is most important. Regardless of the type you choose, dealing with pent up emotions is essential to building up resilience.

Journal – Keeping everything bottled up inside takes its toll, even the small things add up. Writing down your thoughts, feelings, and ideas each day, can release a lot of pent up frustration and can be very enlightening. *Side tip* - make a BITCH journal! I met a wise woman who kept 2 journals. One for her everyday thoughts and the other purely to rant and get anything she wanted to release off her chest. I thought this was a brilliant tip! Just make sure it is kept well hidden. LOL

Family & Friends - You can tell yourself you don't need anyone but learning to handle life's bumpy roads requires some hand holding and shoulders to lean on along the way. Human beings need social interaction to thrive. A simple reminder from a friend that they have been thinking about you can do amazing things to lift your spirits. Just don't forget how important face to face communication is. Get out there! Join a special interest group through *Meetup*, take a fitness class, chat with the person next to you in line for coffee etc. There are lots of ways to connect with people.

Evaluate your relationships – Decide if the people in your life are worth taking up your valuable time. Does interacting with this person tend to lift your spirits or drag you down? Do you feel good about yourself when you are around them? Do they have a positive outlook? If you offer support and express an interest in their life, do they reciprocate? You don't have to cut ties completely with those who have a negative influence but take them out of your close circle. To build up resilience, the best thing you can do is surround yourself with a positive, supportive social community. Who knows, you may even have a little fun along the way!

Forgive past grievances – Whether with family, friends or colleagues, make a conscious choice to deal with any issues and not just sweep them under the carpet. These hidden resentments build up and drain your available reserve of resilience to deal with future issues that may arise. Ask yourself what purpose holding onto this grudge has, if any? It's only hurting you in the end. Forgiveness is a very hard thing to swallow but the benefits are huge.

Personal Development – Keep working to train your brain into believing it can and will overcome anything.

Build Confidence - Build confidence in who you are and what you can do! My experience has proved my mind is my most powerful force. Our actions are completely influenced by our beliefs and if you don't believe you can, you simply won't. Be confident that with the right strategies you WILL get through this – even STRONGER than before!

Change Your Mindset - Change your mindset. See the glass as half full instead of half empty. When struggling, step back. Try to see it from an alternate, positive standpoint? What is the purpose behind this? Perhaps there is something to be learned? If still cloudy, make a list of pros and cons. If you are ambitious, go one step further and brainstorm potential solutions. This process trains your brain to start processing obstacles less harshly, as part of life's path of discovery. Another advantage is positive people attract positive people – law of attraction. Who wants to be around a Negative Nelly? And this positive interaction is a key ingredient to building up your resilience. Start by wearing a smile when you can. It's contagious.

Gratitude and & Giving Back - Make gratitude a part of your daily routine. When you start to appreciate what you have, even the little things can make your life seem a lot better. This can be integrated into your journaling. Write down at least 3 things you are grateful for each day. Writing it down helps it stick in our minds and remember what we are grateful for. NO ONE IS JUDGING! Go beyond the obvious family, health, and home responses. It can be as small as getting the concert tickets you wanted. Only you are ever going to read it.

Help others – Donate to charity, buy a coffee for the person behind you in line, help an elderly person carry something, or plan a surprise meal for your spouse. Helping and giving to others has the dual effect of making both the receiving party and us feel special. This in turn lowers our stress levels, building up our resilience a little further with the belief that we are deserving of good things happening in the future.

Physical Environment – This can be described as anything that our senses can physically experience like touch, smell, sight, hearing, and/or taste. Create a space and spend time in places that make you feel happy and at peace. Perhaps a walk, sitting in the garden, reading by a fire or candlelight etc.

De-clutter or make some changes to ensure your home is a welcoming place. You spend most of your time there so it should be a safe, comforting space.

Mindful Stress Test -Walk into your home, immediately notice your body. Did any parts of it tense up as you walked in? What about your breath and heart rate? Did either elevate? If so, perhaps it's time to examine what's at the core of that stress within the home itself.

Spirituality - Meditation comes in many forms and is easily available anywhere, anytime, at any cost. Try just sitting still and paying attention to your thoughts. Your subconscious mind can tell you so much. Really tuning into what your body is telling you can release a great deal of stress.

Mindfulness can be practiced with or without meditation. According to the Merriam-Webster Dictionary, mindfulness is *the practice of maintaining a nonjudgmental state of heightened or complete awareness of one's thoughts, emotions, or experiences on a moment-to-moment basis.*

Research has linked mindfulness practice with less stress and anxiety, more focus, better sleep, managed chronic pain, less depression and more.

Similar to the test above, try simply pausing when you feel

strong emotions to notice how it feels in your body – like tightness in your jaw and shoulders when you feel stress, warmth in your chest when you feel love, and butterflies in your stomach when you feel nervous.

Fun & Recreation – It's so much easier to overcome life's struggles when we take time out for some fun! It's important to train our brains to notice the good times.

Celebrate the mini successes in each day! - Was today a little less painful than yesterday? Did you accomplish something you never thought you could? Celebrate with something you love like dinner at your favorite restaurant, seeing a play, etc.

Unplug - Unplug by going out and having some fun. Take some risks! It takes practice to move out of your comfort zone, but you will be glad you did. I am not saying you should bet your house at the casino or climb Mt. Everest, but if you always wanted to bungee jump, take salsa lessons, or swim with a dolphin – go for it! Life is precious and it's meant to be fully lived with whatever time we have. Look at some of the most successful people. They did not get there without taking risks and making significant changes. Speaking of changes...

You MUST Accept CHANGE to Build Resilience.

I am a true testament that change and difficult times build resilience. Looking out my condo window at the gorgeous cityscape, I am astonished at how my life has transformed over the last 5 years. I never could have imagined that I could be happy in this situation. From a 20-year marriage, raising 2 girls with a good life on all accounts, to overcoming a debilitating condition, a marriage breakup, a house disaster, and a total career change. It's hard to be grateful for some of these changes but I am happy they happened as I feel I am in the best stage of my life and I no longer fear the unknown. It's exciting to not always be able to predict what's coming.

Changes come in all forms. Some are positive like a promotion, and some difficult like disease. During the hardest times, allowing myself to go through the following stages in order to heal and accept the new changes in my life was integral to building my resilience.

Grief - Accept the sadness and cry it out, watch a tearjerker movie if you have to.
Anger - Why did this happen to me? Release in any way that works for you (i.e. exercise, hitting a pillow, writing etc.) if it's not hurting anyone else.
Forgiveness – Resentment will only drag you down further.
Acceptance – the changes that have occurred in your life and those that still need to happen.
Determination – to overcome these obstacles and make this the best life it can be!

Key Takeaways:

- Success does not happen without change.
- We need to fail in order to learn, so go ahead and try.
- Life would be very boring if nothing ever changed.

- The changes we dread often lead to some of the greatest things in life.
- Don't resist those that are presented to you as something miraculous may occur…. even better – seek them out!

Through Adversity Comes Transformation – Welcome to a Wonderful New Life!

Although the past 5 years were the most challenging of my life, I would not change them. So transformational, it's mind-blowing! My entire life has evolved in ways I never dreamed of. One would almost think that destiny played a part and that my life at that time needed a little shaking up. Regardless, I stand here today, proud of who I have become. Someone I believe my girls can look up to, and someone, through the power of resilience and adaptation to change, is not afraid to face the world head on.

"Every mountain top is in reach if you just keep climbing."
– Barry Finlay

About Alison Verge

It took a major health crisis and a 20-year marriage break-up for Alison Verge to truly discover resilience, the importance of change and eventually her true calling of becoming a Relationship and Dating Coach. Leaving her former 25-year Client Relationship/Account Management career behind, determined to make every moment count and her daughters proud, Alison aims to make a difference in this world by helping others find, keep and cherish lasting love through her Path2Love Coaching practice. You can find out more about Alison here: www.path2love.com

IMPLEMENTING BOUNDARIES

by Pleasant Smith

"People come into your life for a reason, a season, or a lifetime. When you figure out which one it is, you will know what to do for each person."
– Author unknown

After many years of life experiences plus listening to others talk about their story and their perception of life, their wants, and their needs, there is one thing that I learned. If you keep living your life to please everyone else, you are at risk of losing yourself. We are all created uniquely different. We do not think or act the same way. It doesn't matter what our culture or environment are like. Each person's views on life will be different, so how can anyone show up 100% for another person? No one can.

I can remember coaching one of my female clients who labeled herself a people pleaser. When I asked her why she thought she was a people pleaser, she gave evidence of what she had been doing in her relationships. During our sessions, I learned that it went back to her childhood. I asked her whether or not she had done anything to try to change this pattern and if she was doing anything now. But what stood out to me was her wanting to end the pain she was feeling. Although in reality she was wearing thin emotionally, physically, and mentally, her motivation to change was her children, her two teenage boys, and her daughter. She was balancing work and being a single parent. No one seemed to realize that she had a lot on her plate because whenever they would call on her, she would show up. She tried to make herself available for everyone and every event.

We designed a plan for her transformation with a clear intention of implementing boundaries starting with two basic but crucial pillars. Beginning with her *'no, consistently means no,'* in order for her yes to have value. We all should be mindful of this. Whatever is always available we tend to take for granted. Unfortunately, we only realize its importance when it is no longer available.

If you find yourself doing more when you have already done all that you can for someone and they are still asking for more, then it is time for you to refocus your attention where it matters most...on you.

We were created to adapt but fueling the fire is not the approach. You need to bring the heat down. Giving a person more of what they already use for comfort will only allow them to be more comfortable, not appreciative. It is understandable for us to want to be liked and accepted but sometimes things don't happen as we have hoped, which causes disappointment. This might lead to fear, frustration, resentment, anger, malice, and mistrust, but in my opinion, the number one is guilt. Reflecting on past experience, there's always something we wish we could have done differently. It's not that easy. The past is the past and we can't change it.

We were raised to put others first. We were told to accept life as it is, to blend in because if we didn't, we might push people away or hurt their feelings. For instance, can you recall a time you didn't want to go somewhere but you felt pressured to do so? Or perhaps you didn't find a guy attractive and your friends tried to convince you how nice he was, labeling you as unreasonable? Now this roles over into the present causing you to doubt yourself, overlooking the need to implement boundaries. Therefore, the way we live our life and the outcome we have in our relationships depends on how grounded we are when it comes to making our boundaries clear, especially in our intimate or close relationships.

The most important reason for boundaries is for your own benefit and thus should be implemented in accordance with your personal outcome in mind.

So, knowing what your boundaries are and putting them into practice helps you to communicate them easily. If you don't, even the kindest person, your friends, or partner won't be able to respect those boundaries.There is a saying: *Do unto others have you would have them done unto you.* But that has since been changed. It is now *Do unto others as they want you to do unto them*. I believe this to be true. You teach others how you would want to be treated.

A safe place to start is with your immediate family. It is ok to ask for what you need in a relationship. Trust that your partner will hear what you are saying and be willing to work with you with love. If this is difficult for you, ask yourself why it is hard to do. What comes up for you? What really is hindering you? What would be the outcome if you set a boundary? When dealing with issues, keep in mind that it might not be solved right away but you could settle for a compromise or at times even a loss. This is important to take into consideration. It should come from a place of mutual balance.

As individuals we came together to form a partnership. Each has his/her own characteristics in a relationship to make it work. Not everything will be compatible. Acknowledge the other person's contribution. Try not to judge or criticize. The boundaries that are put in place should be a guideline like a GPS system for both people to navigate in a fulfilling relationship journey.

Invite each day as another day to learn something new about making your relationship work.

Don't be afraid to speak up out of concern or for clarity, it is necessary for a strong foundation. It is a new space-filling up with positive boundaries and clear communication on your requirements, needs, and wants in a relationship.Being clear on what you would or wouldn't tolerate will come across as being genuine to your partner and not defensive or arrogant. This forms trust but first, check your self-esteem. Be in the present and experience that feeling. If you feel uncomfortable, he will certainly feel it too. You should know yourself in such a way, having the confidence to understand

and appreciate the response of the other person. If they agreed or disagreed with you, it is okay. Knowing what you want is what you will be able to give also. You should have that relationship you dreamt of with your significant other, by starting the groundwork with self-love, curiosity, excitement, honesty, trust, intimacy, joy and happiness.

Avoid controlling the outcome. Just be in the moment. Experience creating wonderful memories. The only thing a person really has control over is to create an experience of life happenings. Having the freedom to be authentic with your boundaries is a wonderful thing because your physical, emotional, mental, spiritual, and financial status are all a part of the effect of having boundaries.

Make a list or create your own chart to get clarity on boundaries that you need to implement growth for a healthy relationship for you and your partner by using the six topics mentioned (mental, physical, emotional, spiritual and financial).

One advantage of getting what you want by implementing boundaries is that it can be done any time in the relationship. It is a change that is doable by having a laser focus. It is not impossible. Being consistent with a firmer stand might be necessary to end being taken for granted and to stop being complacent. A radical approach might be needed. A person only knows what they know, this comes about with awareness which comes through learning. Don't let up on being disciplined. In the end, you have a choice to accept or reject certain behaviors. You have a choice of who you have in your space and what you want or do not want. You have a choice in how to use your time and energy. Having choices is the most important gift given to us. So, when the time comes to implement your boundaries, be radical. You owe it to yourself to do it with ease.

Your beliefs, your thinking, and your attitude makes you who you are. It's personal and should be accepted and vice versa. So, whenever you and your partner can't seem to agree on an issue, take the time to hear them out. Seek to be understood before you can understand. Emotional behaviors control the way an issue is dealt with and trigger points may control the outcome. But this must be recognized with different types of feelings coming up and this must be addressed so an understanding may form. Whatever the issues may be, owning responsibility is always a factor.

Another thing is to speak your truth as much as possible instead of making excuses to protect the other person's feelings. Practice letting go and the other person will handle their feelings. When speaking the truth be authentic.

Feeling forced to go somewhere with friends on a night when you would rather stay home? Simply say why you would prefer not to accompany them. Your genuine friends will understand.

Finally, get a support system. It might be that one friend who understands and sticks around through the changes you are making. It might be your partner or coach or social group who holds you accountable in this process. Someone is always willing and able to assist. Changes do not come easy; it takes a lot of effort and a lot more support to have that drive to stay grounded with your intention to achieve happiness and success. Don't ever be afraid to do what feels good to you. Be disciplined in achieving your happiness, your peace of mind, and your prosperity knowing that your path will always be crossed by others. But one certainty is you will always be the forefront of your life. Relationships are a constant journey, not a destination. Trust that you're in the driver's seat of your life and you have a firm grip on the steering wheel.

About Pleasant Smith

Pleasant Smith loves and enjoys all areas of her professional life as a Relationship Coach, a Podcaster, and an Author. She strives to excel in her career with a driven intention....her passion to serve.

She has never lost sight of her most fulfilling purposes in life, the joy of raising her daughter and three sons. She lives in Connecticut in that serenity mood that inspired her to write. You can find out more about Pleasant here: https://www.facebook.com/Due.coaching40/?modal=admin_todo_tour

HOW TO GET UNSTUCK
by Pleasant Smith

"In the process of healing, it involves treating yourself with care and concern, self-kindness, self-compassion, mindfulness, and self-worth. Be brave and stand for what you believe in even if you stand alone."
– Author unknown

I really love this quote as it's a powerful reminder that your experience in life is yours, whatever, whenever or wherever you may never forget that self worth is very important.

Changes are an inevitable part of life, your present might represent the past, but it doesn't have to define the future.

We all have the gift of choice. So, we can choose to turn our problems into possibilities and have the freedom for a better understanding of tomorrow. Although self-love seems simple, and it is just a two-word topic, it could be tied to a list of subtopics. Simply because anyone could or should understand it and most importantly make it a priority, unfortunately, it isn't so.

So here is the thing. One of the reasons why we may stay stuck could be from the absence of, or not taking notice of self-love. At times we have no one to hold us accountable, we constantly ignore how important and necessary it is to take our complete well-being seriously. We struggle with this need for a couple of reasons. As we move through life, we have developed routines and operate on autopilot, caring for everyone before ourselves. Then life happens and we get hurt and we end up in the victim space, a constant mood, ultimately forgetting that we are our first priority and also our best caregiver.

If you ever felt there was something holding you back from achieving your vision, robbing you of your happiness and living a passion-filled life that you would love to live, here's how to make the change.

Stop Being The Victim

What does your day-to-day life look like regarding dealing with issues and others? Give yourself permission to notice or recognize a pattern that you've adopted towards pain/hurt. Try to avoid making excuses out of every challenging situation and take full responsibility for your actions. Avoid wearing your past hurt as a branded tattoo as a reminder for everyone to see. There is no sense in staying in a bad situation that makes you suffer. Be proactive and take action. This could be the start of a change; the beginning for a new life.

Fantasy vs Reality

What is your strategy on escaping? Do you find that most of the time you are reliving the past but only in your head?

Are you reminiscing on past events, times and dates? Here is another option:

Draw a Venn diagram with fantasy on one side and reality on the other. In the fantasy circle write your thoughts from the past; the should haves and could haves. Now on the reality side, write down your thoughts about what you deserve. Finally, in the middle where the circles intersect, write an action plan of how you are going to love and care for yourself.

Fantasy is a comfort zone that a lot of people find themselves in because they are afraid of change; the fear that they might encounter problems causing their life to become more difficult. Putting your thoughts on paper will help you to confront what is really going on. This process gives you a tangible view so that you can try to make clear what is in front of you. It causes you to slow down and take notice, and if it is hard to grasp at first, that means you are on the right path. Changes definitely need to happen.

Clean Up Confrontation Cobwebs

As an adult I have found myself battling with low self-esteem from time to time and not being able to trust, which causes me to make poor choices in relationships. This leads to frustration, resentment, and loneliness. It seems as if I'm living in a deja vu. So, I tried to show up differently each time but I wasn't in alignment physically or mentally. My mind and my emotions were off. I hadn't realized that I was pretending. In fact, I was so broken that I didn't even know the real me, and for each failed relationship, I would blame the other person. I didn't know what to do, how to do it, or even why. But my relationships just kept spiraling out of control.

Whenever you're feeling disconnected, you need a transparent conversation with yourself. What are you telling yourself? Or is it someone else's voice you're hearing? How far back is your recollection of it because what the mind does is remind us. It is quick to go into that filing cabinet and pull out old records as proof that what we are thinking is backed by evidence. No matter what experience we had in the past or what our present circumstances may look like, the main culprit holding us hostage is our mind. It has proof to back our theory/thinking and that is where we need to start the process of getting unstuck. By refiling the cabinet and shredding the content that only serves as fear.

Cleaning up the present is great but understanding the root will bring about real changes.

Live Up to Your Expectation

A few years later, I had made a significant shift through working with a relationship coach. It was because of her teachings I could identify areas in my life that needed urgent attention. Inner work needed to be done on myself but, most importantly, that breakthrough was realizing it was about me first; that everything started with me. If I want changes, it has to start from within. No amount of blaming and complaining will make the cut unless I take responsibility for my life and the outcome that I envision.

This wasn't easy to absorb at first let alone understand but, I was compelled to stay with her teachings.

Normally you can't correct something unless you see that there is a need to. If you recognize that you're doing the same thing over and over and getting the same result, or someone keeps pointing out to you that there is an area in your life that you need to work on, then you owe it to yourself to take the time to pay attention. Alone time for a lot of us is loneliness and isolation, but the most effective way of using this period of your life is to understand who you are through meditation and reflection. Undisturbed times and quiet moments are privileges we should not take lightly. If we are true to ourselves and want to improve our own lives, these are opportunities to do so.

We grow up in a culture where others are telling us what to do from the time, we are children and we do not learn how to make our own choices. I have seen countless lives being dictated by others' opinions on how they should be living, which causes relationship contamination. I am talking about adults who cannot function without simple guidelines of someone telling them what to do. Getting clarity of when, how, why, and what is keeping you stuck is the key formula to you having your breakthrough.

Prioritize Each Transitional Moment

Fear is a feeling that everybody has at some time or another around a situation or in life in general but, it is not the real problem that keeps you stuck. The source is the reason for the fear that keeps one stuck. There is nothing wrong with being afraid and still moving forward. It is the baby steps that count; it is motion in play that makes things happen. I have learned and understood that everything serves a purpose. Try to see a situation for what it is but also be curious of what it is revealing to you. To win at anything there must be a strategy to accomplish it, an intention. So, there must be a starting point. You must know what you want and envision the end so you can be fully committed to doing the work and make the time and effort for your success.

Being successful at anything feels good, a great feeling for that matter, and that's how constructive people think and work. They set goals and accomplish them.

In order for you to get unstuck, it is the goals that you set which will get you into action. Nothing will get done if there isn't some work happening. Remember practice makes perfect. How do you know you're on a successful path? How do you know that things are in motion? You know and understand when your whole being is in it. Try to be fully engaged. Focus on the part that keeps you interested and causes a sense of fulfillment. Let this motivate you to show up with a positive attitude. This should apply to your personal and social life as well as your business. If a door opens, take the chance to experience new experiences. Have the mindset that there is always something to do to improve your life. Keep your eyes on the prize. Continue to set tangible goals and knock them out. This will keep you focused and improve your awareness of your purpose.

Make a Deposit in Your Emotional Piggy Bank

Everyone was created to experience physical, emotional, mental, and spiritual health. So many of us ignore the importance of having all of them in play all the time for an easier safer way to navigate through life. You need all four of them for guidance and protection through life. For example, after you break off a relationship you might still think about the person all the time. You might feel empty, sad, confused, and lonely. We might not recognize it, but our spirit is the only force that keeps guiding and protecting us in this moment. I have heard more than once, "I don't know how I got through that time, or that situation." We know, but we don't give ourselves enough credit because it is not tangible.

We tend to hide our emotions from ourselves and from others. We ignore how important it is and how it really impacts our lives and the lives of those around us.

We criticize ourselves. We see ourselves as competing with others instead of allowing ourselves to have those experiences and opportunities in challenges rather than competition.

Be aware when you are short on self-compassion. Instead, try a little tenderness. Release any pent-up energy. Forgive yourself and others who you think have wronged you. Everybody makes mistakes. Get rid of the attachment to the past. Doing things in different and new ways makes life more interesting and satisfying.

Live a Life Well-Loved

What is the benefit of letting go and releasing? How would that make you feel; happiness, freedom, peace-of-mind, independence?

There could be sacrifices that you would not want to make but would be worth your time because the why is bigger and better. When you measure it short term or long term there should be no regrets. You get rid of negative habits and build new and positive habits. What is required is a strong desire to persevere and an open mind for possibilities. The end game is a more confident and inspired you who is showing up more fully to serve yourself and others who are depending on you. That feeling you get knowing that you're special and you don't need anyone to tell you because you feel fulfilled, expanded and purposeful.

Self-improvement also means developing a better life including will-power, self-discipline, concentration, and inner peace. As you move forward to reset your mind; to strive to enjoy every moment of your life no matter what you're doing, even as circumstances and situations change, it is easier said than done but what is most rewarding is not giving up. Understand this, a ship that throws an anchor cannot sail. It must raise the anchor first, and so it is in your life. For you to move on you need to raise the anchor, your attachment to the past. Be disciplined. Stay on course. It might not be what you were expecting but you will be alright.

About Pleasant Smith

Pleasant Smith loves and enjoys all areas of her professional life as a Relationship Coach, a Podcaster, and an Author. She strives to excel in her career with a driven intention....her passion to serve.

She has never lost sight of her most fulfilling purpose in life, the joy of raising her daughter and three sons. She lives in Connecticut in that serenity mood that inspired her to write. You can learn more about Pleasant here: https://www.facebook.com/Due.coaching40/?modal=admin_todo_tour

SELF LOVE IS CREATING GOALS

by Nancy White

*"You are never too old to set another goal or to
dream a new dream."*
– C. S. Lewis

Only YOU can choose your goals. Others can be an influence, positive or negative. In the end, our choices and actions enable us to accomplish our goals. Creating goals, taking action steps, and accomplishing your goals are the best self-love habits that you can have. Goals come in all sizes: small, like getting your teeth brushed before leaving for the day, and big, like being healthy and financially prepared before retirement, and everything in between.

Why is setting goals so important?

Goals are the things you want to accomplish in life, and yes, goals can and do change as we age. Not setting goals is like a small boat out to sea without a rudder or navigation system, being tossed to and fro at the mercy of the waves. That's the way some people live their lives. How do you think you will evolve into becoming the best version of you that you and others will love?

You evolve into becoming the best version of you by creating and achieving new and ongoing goals. When you focus on progress and not perfection, you can break down a goal into manageable steps. It allows you to tackle your dreams while balancing the mountains and valleys of daily life. When you create new and ongoing goals, you can make choices each day to take action steps towards completing your goals. Remind yourself, you are accomplishing either "good," "better," or "best" actions, without attaching any negative self judgement. Every action step is a step closer, whether a baby or giant step.

Goals can be a tool to guide you to accomplishments and success, but you must move beyond the theoretical and notebook of lists to experience your outcome. Scheduling time to disconnect and create space and time to think and connect with yourself is awesome. Writing down your goals is excellent. These are awesome starting points, but how do you even decide on what goals you want to accomplish? I'm glad you asked!

Let's start with the priority goal – You!

Love yourself today just as you are, after all we are not guaranteed tomorrow.

Schedule "me" time in your calendar. How about a bubble bath with candles and relaxing music? Schedule a massage, turn-off your phone and do some fun things you enjoy....... Now that is radical love!

When you look in the mirror, focus on the positive things you like about yourself, not the things you want to change.

Affirm your positive attributes. Literally out loud affirm yourself. For example, "You have beautiful, healthy teeth, hair, skin or strong muscles, and a great sense of humor that makes people laugh. You have a kind, loving heart that makes others feel accepted."

Set boundaries. You know yourself and your responsibilities. No and no thank you are great words, or 'I think someone else may be better suited at this time.' Being overcommitted only adds stress to your life and puts you on a path to emotional and physical burnout.

Allow self-love to become part of your ongoing lifestyle. Explore what inspires you, refreshes you, and yes even makes you happy. Different seasons of life place varying demands on you, but no matter what the season, if you don't show up for yourself and find ways to love and care for yourself, then you are missing out on the abundance that could be in that season.

Now that the priority goal is established, let's check out some other important goals and ways to accomplish them.

Identify

First, schedule a time to be alone in a quiet place. Turn off technology for ten minutes or more. Get paper and a pen to write down your thoughts.

Ponder what is important to you in life.

Is there a theme or common topic or word that keeps bubbling to the surface?

What areas of your life need a "tune-up," realignment, or make-over? (health, family, business, finances, friends, travelling, home, etc.) Be specific about what you desire. Don't limit yourself due to self-limiting beliefs or variables out of your control. Focus on what is possible.

Review what you have written and narrow down the list to things you couldn't live without. Re-write your list and clarify your top 3 areas that are most important to you. Now take a couple of minutes and think how achieving these changes will affect your life. Who else will these changes affect, now and in the future?

The Plan

The next step is creating a plan using the Simpleology System (used by the military). I refer to the plan as the reverse engineering method. This is a time you can always ask someone you like and trust to help you brainstorm your plan creation. Identify one goal at a time and then start the reverse action steps. Be as detailed as possible, every action step will affect the next step of accomplishing your goal.

Example:

Goal – Eating a yummy, crunchy organic peanut butter and organic black cherry jam on organic sprouted grain soft bread sandwich.

Reverse the steps – start at the bottom. Your action steps will have dates. This is just an example:

- Enjoy eating your delicious sandwich. You may need a glass of water or cold milk to go with it.
- Spread desired amount of crunchy peanut butter on 1 of the 2 slices of bread. Next, spread the desired amount of black cherry jam on the other slice of bread and put the 2 slices of bread together.
- Open the jars of crunchy organic peanut butter and organic black cherry jam. Open the bread bag and take out 2 slices of bread and put them on the plate.
- Get out a clean plate and a butter knife.
- Wash your hands.
- Drive home from the grocery store. Remove groceries from the grocery bag and put them on the kitchen counter.
- Drive to the grocery store and buy crunchy organic peanut butter, organic black cherry jam and organic sprouted grain soft bread.
- Get in and start your car.
- Think I would like a peanut butter and jam sandwich.
- Work to earn money to buy groceries.

This may seem silly but putting the steps down to achieve your goals can be as simple or complex as you choose.

Accountability

Do you agree that we let ourselves "off the hook", procrastinate, slide by, or make excuses? Whatever the reason, we just don't get "it" done. This is where an accountability partner is so valuable and will be a great asset to help you reach your goals. Yes, we all do better when we have someone else cheering us on and wanting us to succeed, agree? Guess what? You can have more than one accountability partner or a mentor for different areas of your life. The person(s) should have your best interest at heart and have a clear understanding about your goals, steps, and dates. Mutually decide when and how weekly or bi-weekly check-ins will be made. Use check-ins for progress updates or adjustments as needed. Consider having a mutually beneficial accountability partner where each of you shares your goals with steps and dates to be met. Keep calls short and consistent, and have a way to measure your progress.

3 D's: Doable, Dates, and Deadlines

Dates should be realistic and doable taking into consideration other people that may be needed to complete your action steps. Life happens and if dates are not met, just keep going and reset the completion date. Stopping to reassess is positive and very beneficial. Keep an open mind and heart to adjust if needed.

These are the times when having an accountability partner will encourage you not to give up or stop. Celebrate each action step accomplished along the way. Put a smiley sticker on the day of the calendar or in your notebook as you complete each step. Yes, you can jump up and down, pat yourself on the back, be like the little pink energizer bunny, keep on going……

Out of Sight, Out of Mind

Print out your goals, write them on sticky notes, create a vision board, or create a screensaver for your computer or, better still, your phone! Be sure you can see your goals every day. Use the reminder on your phone or google calendar to schedule your action steps to keep you on track; whatever it takes to see your goals. Remember out of sight, out of mind!

Your Why

Why does it matter for you to achieve your goals? If there is no emotion attached to successfully achieving your goals, it will probably not happen. Go back to the beginning, why is this goal so important? When roadblocks, slowdowns, or disappointments happen, stop and remember why this goal is important and who it will affect when you succeed?

Recap

- IDENTIFY
- THE PLAN
- ACCOUNTABILITY
- 3 D's DOABLE DATES AND DEADLINES
- OUT OF SIGHT OUT OF MIND
- BELIEF?

Fast Fun Facts

- Writing down goals makes you 42% more likely to achieve them and when you share them in writing with someone who believes in you (accountability partner) you are even more likely to achieve your goals. When you write down your goals you are using both sides of your brain. - Huff Post

- People who journal daily have a higher success rate in experiencing positive changes in their lives.
- A lot of people love using this acronym - SMART Goals. SMART means Specific, Measurable, Attainable, Realistic and Time-sensitive.
- I came across this intriguing self-challenge experiment to share with you – Each morning for the next seven days, start your day by writing down your goals and dreams in the four key areas of life:

  1. Health
  2. Love & relationships
  3. Vocation
  4. Time & money freedom

- Don't write down what you THINK you can have, or what seems possible under your current circumstances... Instead, write down what you'd truly LOVE, no matter how big or bold it may seem to you right now. What will happen when you do this experiment?

- While this experiment is simple, it's also very powerful, and it will cause two things to happen:

  1. The first thing that happens is you'll reach a new level of clarity concerning your goals and dreams. The act of writing your goals down requires a

level of clarity that just thinking about them doesn't and this then communicates, "I mean business. I'm serious about this. This matters to me. It's my life."

2. Next, you will shift what you focus on throughout your day, including your awareness about opportunities that are right in front of you, but that often can't be seen under normal circumstances.

No matter what processes you use to obtain your goals, remember it is one step at a time. If you get stuck or sidetracked, reach out to your accountability partner. Celebrate the steps you are making and really celebrate reaching each goal.

Self-love creates new goals, and never stops...

> *"You are never too old to set another goal*
> *or to dream a new dream."*
> *– C. S. Lewis*

Bonus: Scientific benefits of journaling
#1: Journaling can reduce depression and anxiety.
#2: Journal writing can help boost immune function.
#3: Journaling helps cultivate gratitude.
#4: Journaling can help with recovery from trauma.
#5: Keeping a journal can improve memory function

I would love to hear from you! What have been your successes and your challenges in creating your new goals?

About Nancy White

Nancy White wants to live in a world where people will thrive and not just survive both physically and financially. Her business is to assist health conscious adults in creating their healthy lifestyles they can tweak as they age.

Nancy has a natural gift for connecting people, especially in business. She has served as the Foundation leader for eWomen Network and established the first Heart Link Network for women in Charlotte.

She is the author of, The G.R.T. Journal, an Amazon Best Seller and Light at The End of the Funnel volume 2, an international Amazon Best Seller. Nancy is one of the Hosts & Executive Producers of The Network Show, launched August 2019. She has been cultivating her Healthy Cells Chick business since 2007 making a difference in assisting people in creating their healthy lifestyles.

www.thehealthycellschick.com

COMFORT ZONE - BE A F.E.A.R. REBEL
by Crystal Cockerham

*"Sometimes we have to step out of our comfort zones.
We have to break the rules. And we have to discover
the sensuality of fear. We need to face it,
challenge it, dance with it."*
– Kyra Davis

The Kyra Davis quote is a recent find for me. It captured my attention immediately. For me, what popped into my head when I first read it was, *be a rebel, a fear rebel.* Ah, yes, now you are intrigued. I invite you to play with this perspective yourself as you read on. Just like with anything, it's best to start at the beginning and this chapter is about comfort zones. Are you ready to dive in?

"Comfort zone" is a really silly term in the personal growth and spiritual development realms. It's very name, comfort zone, is deceiving. If a counselor, coach, mentor, spiritual guide or teacher has ever said you are in your comfort zone, what they are really saying is, "You have become very comfortable in fear, sadness, living small, not giving yourself a chance, etc." Now, does THAT sound like a comfort zone you want to stay in? I didn't think so.

When was the last time you stretched yourself? I mean

really stretched and stepped outside your comfort zone? I bet it has been a while or maybe you have never really stepped beyond it at all. You may have just stretched from high school to college, from your parents' house to your own place, from being single to in a relationship, or chose the local job vs. the one that would mean relocation. You get the idea, choosing to always play it safe vs. taking a chance on you and your dreams.

What if I told you your comfort zone is a myth; a sugar-coated illusion your ego has placed in your consciousness in order to stay in control, to keep you in fear and from growing into your truest & highest self, the you you are destined to become?

It's true! Your comfort zone really isn't comfortable, it's just what you are used to. Ego likes the known and fears the unknown. That is true too! No matter how wonderful or hurtful for you the unknown is, ego will keep you from exploring either in equal measure because the outcome is unpredictable.

We all have ego. We need it. Its job is to keep us safe. When ego steps in, takes control and stays in control, that is when struggle, resistance, hurt & lack of fulfillment happen. No matter how unappealing that all sounds, I just described the spiritual definition of a comfort zone.

When we find ourselves in a space of discomfort or dis-ease in our life, it is because the part of us that is evolving and changing is quite literally in a stand-off with that part that wants nothing to do with change. Our ego is happy being in control, in the know. It finds a false sense of security in maintaining the status quo, a.k.a. comfort zone, and conspires in every way to avoid change.

You see your ego is your most faithful and dependable soldier. So faithful, so dependable, so good at strategy that it is your own personal general. It is in charge of maintaining the comfort zone. No matter who or what attempts to burst that bubble, ego is going to do everything possible to distract you from it. No matter how appealing or how much you desire it.

Let me give you an example of what a covert mastermind your faithful general is. Years ago, I happened upon a book. I remember it like it was yesterday. I was still in college at the time. It was one of my trips to Borders, my favorite place to go, do some research, and work on papers. When I found this particular book, there was no question, I was buying it. It was obvious when I purchased it that it would go onto my stack of books, I had on reserve for studying in between semesters. Some time passed and I had picked the book up a couple of times and started reading it, but for whatever reason I just never finished it.

Fast forward a few years, I reacquaint myself with the book, still having a strong desire to read it. However, every time I picked it up I would suddenly come down with a headache or my eyes would start crossing and I was suddenly very tired. Mind you, this isn't a massive book or a boring book by any stretch. My college studies had turned me into an avid reader. (Seriously, I read all four Twilight books in 6 days with three active kids.) Anyway, this continued for quite some time. One day I ran into a life coach and we struck up a conversation. Long story short, that was when I first heard of ego. My stubbornness outwilled my ego and I finished the book. I have learned a lot more about ego since that time!

Nine years later, that book was a life changer for me. I went on to do a program of study with the author, have since purchased more of her books, and I look forward to attending some of her live events too! You see that book led me to remember both my purpose as well as awakening ancient past-life wisdom within me. How can you get more positive than that?

Ego had no idea how profound and positive the effects of that book were going to be for me, it just knew it wasn't a known outcome and kept deterring me to keep its comfort zone intact. I had to take the reins back and consciously manage my energy and make my own decision to step outside of that comfort zone.

Now doesn't it sound amazing to leave behind a state of being that consisted of headaches and sudden onsets of exaggerated sleepiness? Although at the time I didn't know it was an act of self-love to overcome my comfort zone. It very much was.

I have since busted through the barriers of many other comfort zones in order to become the me I am today. Oh, there are and will be more comfort zones to blast through because I know as long as I am on this planet in this lifetime, I will continue to grow and expand into the me I was born to become. And, I choose to do it because I love myself enough to dream big and believe in myself enough to pursue my dreams through practicing radical self- love.

To have and practice radical self-love is to NOT have a comfort zone. It is aligning with your heart & soul and allowing your spirit to guide you into your magic zone in the face of fear. Heck in reference to the Kari Davis quote, be a fear rebel!

That's right, I said be a fear rebel. Seriously, how often do you think you are in fear, and I mean you are in real danger? Not as often as you think, in fact, rarely. When fear shows up. Oftentimes it's F.alse E.vidence A.ppearing R.eal, meaning ego is doing its best to keep you in its comfort zone.

So how do you know if it is fear, 'I'm in danger' fear, or fear, 'false evidence appearing real' fear? Stop. Drop what you're doing and because safety comes first, check in with your surroundings. Are you safe? Did you unknowingly enter into a shady part of town? Did you forget to lock your door? You get the idea. Once you know you are physically safe, take some time with this 'fear' energy and:

F.ace it - Stare it right in the face.
E.xplore it - Give it a good once over. You know, measure it up for size.
A.ccept it - Acknowledge and accept that it is there. Don't act like you don't know, because you do.
R.ise above it. - Rebel! Break down those comfort zone

boundaries by doing everything you possibly can to change your routines. Ego l-o-v-e-s routine!

Seriously, if normally you wake up, go to the bathroom, make your tea/coffee and lunch, then take a shower, change it. Wake up, go to the bathroom, hop right into that shower then enjoy your tea/coffee and make your lunch. As you proceed through your day, change everything you can safely change. Yes, you'll have a couple days of feeling like you are discombobulated, you aren't, ego is.

Now, you are ready to:

F.ace the false evidence appearing real and do
E.verything you possibly can to shift that energy
A.nd
R.ise above the 'fear'.

That's right! Rise above the 'fear' in spite of it being there trying to keep you small. Magic zone full steam ahead!

You are a rebel, a fear rebel. What do rebel's do? F.ace/fight E.verything And Run. Only they aren't running away to ego's comfort zone, they are running right through and away from it and headed right into their own magic zone!

> *"When you come to the end of everything you know,*
> *and then you take one more step,*
> *that's where the magic happens."*
> *– McCall Erickson*

Shift happens, magic happens, GROWTH and TRANSFORMATION happen when you stretch yourself by facing everything and rising anyway! You will rise right into your magic zone!

Now, the magic zone is the place to be! Sometimes you're flying down the hill, sometimes you are struggling to make it up the hill, and sometimes you're just enjoying the ride. Doesn't that sound like radical self-love to you?

You deserve to radically love yourself and to be radically loved. Won't you join the spiritual rebellion and be a F.E.A.R. rebel?

The F.E.A.R. Rebel Training Exercise

Set an intention. Being clear on what you want to shift is vital before you can go through the F.E.A.R. flow exercise. What is it you are no longer comfortable with in your 'comfort zone'? What change, shift, or transformation are you ready to radically love yourself through? The clearer you are the easier it will be to find the direction of your magic zone. What is that specific thing? If you are unsure as to what needs to shift for you, think about this; What dynamic/emotional pattern do you NOT want to find yourself in anymore? Do some reflective work on that, whether it is a nice walk, a soak in the tub or journaling until you distill it down to one clear and concise statement and proceed to the F.E.A.R. flow exercise.

Fear Flow Exercise

F.ace it - What are you staring in the face?

E.xplore it - Give it a good once over. You know, measure it up for size. When did this become your comfort zone? Why did it become part of your comfort zone? What is there for you to re-examine and heal from? What limiting belief is waiting to be transformed into a limitless one?

A.ccept it - Acknowledge and accept that it is there. Don't act like you don't know, because you do. Journaling, sketching, even coloring are good exercises to help accept the past and realize it is in the past and doesn't get to define you or limit you any longer.

R.ise above it - Rebel! Break down those comfort zone boundaries by changing everything in your routine you possibly can. Shifting habits is a large part of this. What habits can you start shifting/changing/removing?

Now, you are ready to:

F.ace the false evidence appearing real and replace it by consciously doing

E.verything you possibly can to shift that energy. Take conscious inspired actions that move you forward in manifesting your intention. What are some consciously inspired actions you can take?

A.nd

R.ise above the 'fear'. That's right, rise above the 'fear' despite it being there trying to keep you small. Move toward your magic zone full steam ahead! Just like with any new sport, exercise, activity, etc., you might fall down. This is okay. You will learn how not to. If it were easy, everyone would be doing it and this book would not exist. When we are struggling to implement new healthy lifestyle choices for ourselves, there is a pearl of wisdom for us to attain before we can truly release the unhealthy state of being. What is the pearl of wisdom you are extracting from all of this? You've got this! You were born to do this!

Fight Songs, Mottos, Mantras & Affirmations: It's time to tap into Hollywood here. Every good movie has a soundtrack with a theme song, what's yours? Every 'soldier' or 'general' has a motto/mantra/affirmation, a positive statement that keeps them going. What's yours?

All rebels have a talisman and some type of uniform. If you like to wear jewelry or love crystals like I do, Amethyst is one of the more popular gems that can help you break habits. Black onyx is another, however it works slightly differently. Both Amethyst and Black Onyx help boost your will power, but Black Onyx helps you tap into your inner strength too! And guess what? If you were to wear them both in jewelry, they match with everything! If you aren't a jewelry person, you can also acquire a tumbled stone of one or both and keep them in your left (feminine side, your side of receiving) pocket.

About Crystal Cockerham

An international best-selling author, Mentor & Feminine Wisdom Teacher, Crystal Cockerham works with women to guide them through the spiritual alchemical process of transformation in order to be liberated from the world's perceptions. Using her own special blend of Spiritual Midwifery, she guides women through the process of transformation, forging & solidifying their innate connection to their inner wisdom, allowing them to access their own truth, empowering them to claim their sovereignty & become the women they are truly meant to be, and thus to live a more connected, joy-filled life. To begin your journey, and find out more, visit: www.WisdomAwakens.com

THE 7 SHORTCUTS TO ECSTATIC SOULMATE ATTRACTION

by Joanna Shakti

Attraction. It's simple and it's not. Every challenge you've ever faced in attracting your soulmate, one who fits with you like a lock and key, arises not from what you're doing but from who you are being. What's happening inside you creates what's happening outside you.

I know that might sound a little airy-fairy, and I can tell you as an Electrical Engineer turned Soul Love Mentor, almost 20 years ago, you'll find no greater truth when it comes to life and love. I know because I fought that truth for years. I truly thought that working hard, doing the right things, and being a good person would bring me amazing love. It doesn't work that way. All I got from all that effort was a divorce, followed by a whole lot of heartache. Until, I finally woke up to real love.

If you're like most of the men and women, from their twenties to their seventies, that I have worked with over the last decade and a half, you spend way too much time unconsciously (and sometimes consciously) twisting yourself into a pretzel trying to make love work.

It seems like attraction should just happen; you show up,

you put yourself out there, they will come right? Not so right.

Before we break down attraction onto a map you can follow to attract and keep your soulmate, let's talk about what a soulmate really is and what Soul Love really means.

What is Soul Love?

When you hear the words "Soul Love" you might conjure up images of magical romance and being swept off your feet. For others, it may touch somewhere deep within the center of your body and spread a warmth that seems to touch every cell and beyond.

At the same time, as much as you might hunger for it, this kind of love scares some people so much that the "humanness" within unknowingly fights and resists it. Others chase after a perception and projection of this love, so desperate to fill the gaping hole within that longs for love.

You can't find this love. You are this love. When you know that fully, then you can find soul-to-soul love.

We cannot measure Soul Love. We cannot identify its qualities. We cannot define it, weigh it, or even see it. It is everything and nothing all at once.

Soul Love happens in the body. Soul Love is an experience. It's something we feel.

To manifest your soulmate, to create a soul-to-soul

relationship, you must awaken and activate the soul love that is you. We too often imagine that "soul love" equals, or is, romantic love, but it's not. Soul Love is the prerequisite, the precursor, the foundation of romantic love.

I call romantic soul love "Loving Soul-to-Soul," which means, "my soul meets your soul and together we make magic." It doesn't mean either of us is perfect, but we love each other anyway, and likely, we love each other even more because of our imperfections.

When soul love activates in you it means that you embrace, express, and embody all of who you are. It's self-love at its finest. It means that you are who you are, warts and all, perfections and imperfections, strengths and weaknesses; and you willingly let another see you in all of that.

Soul Love, when it's awake and active in you, makes confidence, connection, and chemistry effortless. It makes romance come alive. This means becoming available for love, which then means you will actually be able to feel loved by someone else.

I know you may say, "Of course I can feel love. That's why I'm putting all this effort into finding a soulmate, because I have so much love to give." Here's the problem. Those who know they have the most love to share often can't feel it; can't receive it themselves. They hope giving it will help them feel it, but it never happens that way. The experience of soul-to-soul love happens on a two-way giving and receiving street.

Again, I know this because I've lived it. The hole where I wanted love to live was so empty. Deep down, I unconsciously believed that I wasn't worth loving. No amount of love poured into me could ever have been enough to fill that hole because I couldn't receive the love. I couldn't feel it, which is the whole reason the hole existed in the first place. Developing your capacity to feel and receive love prepares you for soul love before you can attract it.

I've heard this story mirrored back to me again and again and again over the years from my clients. They too have discovered the source of love within, which, when overflowing, attracts, ignites, and creates a magical soulmate partnership.

The 7 Shortcuts

When you're trying to get over the last breakup, when you're feeling lonely, when you're hungry for intimacy, it might seem like the perfect time to post your online dating profile or ask your friends about other single people they know. That's actually the worst thing you could do. That's the mistake most singles make, setting themselves up for more disappointment and heartache. It may seem like the fastest route to love, but you'll find it to be an endless loop of heartbreaking detours.

On the other hand, if you'll take a breath, slow down, and take these exact shortcuts, you will dramatically accelerate your journey to attract and connect with your soulmate. You'll probably be shocked by how quickly and easily it happens for you, if you take the time to follow each suggestion. Maybe you've heard the phrase, "Slow down to go fast." That's how Ecstatic Soulmate Attraction works.

Shortcut #1: Activate Soul Love

As you know from our earlier exploration of Soul Love, it all starts with you. It starts with awakening and living in the love that lives in and as you. You might think that finding your soulmate will bring you the love you seek. It's just the opposite. When you find the love you seek, within you, then you can attract someone who will meet you in that love, who can amplify and expand it with you.

When you activate Soul Love within you, you recognize that the most important relationship is the relationship with you, and that the strength of your relationship with yourself actually determines the strength of your relationship with anyone else, and most importantly your soulmate.

Your goal here is to step into a state of Ecstatic Authenticity which means you have a strong and deep relationship with yourself, where you know and express your needs, wants, desires, turn-ons, turn-offs, and boundaries. It means that you know and respect who you are so much, that you are no longer willing to settle, sell yourself out, or twist yourself into a pretzel to find or keep love.

By developing this deep relationship with yourself, you will allow yourself to be imperfect. You will allow yourself to be seen in your greatness and your not-so-greatness. When you let yourself be known for the good, the bad, and the ugly, then and only then, will you actually be available for love. Then and only then, will you fully trust love.

Shortcut #2: Be the One

Once you are available for and trusting of love, now it's time to show up fully as your authentic self. Too often singles worry about doing and saying the right thing on a date. The truth is you actually can't say the wrong thing to your soulmate. The kind of person that can and will create a soul love partnership with you, will love you through your mistakes. They will fall in love with you for being you, not for being who you think they want you to be. They will love you more, and more deeply, for being the raw and real you.

In other words, don't try to be the one they want. That will set you up for disaster because, eventually, you'll go back to being totally you, and they'll wonder who it was they were dating in the first place. Men and women alike have experienced dates, and even girlfriends or boyfriends, saying things like "I don't want kids," or "I like broccoli" or "I don't care where I live," only to find out later that wasn't the whole story. This kind of twisting of the truth will surely undermine the foundation of any relationship.

So, be who you are. Be real. Be authentic. Find out how they respond. If they like it, if they fall in love with the real you, then you have a chance of building a soul partnership. If they don't like how you show up, if they criticize you, if they try to change you, this is not your soulmate. Move on.

Be you and discover if they are the one you want. The key is to feel confident enough to choose, and not to worry about whether you'll be chosen.

Shortcut #3: Clear the Past

As you are activating soul love in you and being the one, you want to make sure the past remains in the past. Many of my new clients sincerely believe that they are done with their past relationships and that it's not affecting their current dating experiences. Then we dig in a little deeper and discover they proactively try to protect themselves from the hurt they experienced in their past relationships. When they honestly look within, they realize they pre-judge the opposite sex based on how past partners behaved. Frequently, being honest with themselves, they admit that they still hold some bitterness, resentment, or hurt from long gone relationships. They know they haven't forgiven past partners for how things turned out. This kind of "baggage" truly blocks you from opening up, attracting, and receiving the love you seek.

Our human minds don't like it when we experience hurt. As a matter of fact, our subconscious will do anything it can to protect us from repeating painful experiences, including unconsciously self-sabotaging, in order to ensure we DON'T manifest our soulmate. Why? Simply because if we find him or her, the risk of getting hurt or "losing" them is too high. Our minds, left unchecked, prefer that we stay alone.

What do you do about this invisible baggage? I recommend doing a Conscious Endings Ritual with any past partner where you have even the slightest bit of hurt, anger, resentment, jealousy, or anything of the sort, remaining in your consciousness.

An effective endings ritual includes five key parts. First, let go of any stored feelings and emotions you might be carrying with you. These will block your manifesting energy. Second, completely forgive your ex for anything they might have done, or not done, that contributed to your hurt feelings. Third, completely forgive you for any way that you contributed to the past relationship pains. (I guarantee you, no matter what they did, you had a part in the challenges. If you can't see that, you may want to keep going deeper in your clearing.) Fourth, you'll want to integrate the lessons and blessings you got from that relationship, no matter how painful they might have been. Last but not least, send your past partner blessings on his or her journey.

The great part is you don't need your past lovers or partners to participate! You can do this completely on your own. It may not seem easy, and for many it's not. However, I recommend doing whatever it takes to clean up the past.

Shortcut #4: Believe in It

As you believe, so it is. While you continue to prepare yourself for Soul Love, you need to pay close attention to another insidious saboteur lying within your belief systems. Ask yourself, what do you believe about dating? What do you believe about men? About women? About love? About relationships?

We build our belief systems based on our past experiences. Unfortunately, we think because one guy didn't treat us well, none will. We begin to believe that because someone cheated, others will too. We start to project things like "men are poor communicators" or "women are too emotional," and none of that is true. At a time when we hurt, we decided, usually unconsciously, that all future loves will treat us the same way. Then that's exactly what we manifest. We have the same experience over and over, reinforcing our insidious beliefs systems.

In an attempt to take care of us, our human mind projects current circumstances into the future, imagining them to be permanent. Thinking life will always be the way it is now establishes a new belief in your consciousness. For example, my dad moved out when my parents divorced and then when my mom would date someone and then breakup, my innocent mind decided that "men weren't reliable." So, because the reality of our lives must match our beliefs, I attracted men I couldn't really rely on. When I changed my beliefs, I met much different men.

I encourage you to dig in and discover your unconscious beliefs and then release anything that isn't supportive of attracting and creating a soul love partnership. Once you do, you'll start attracting much better dating prospects into your life.

Shortcut #5: Establish Polarity

Opposites attract. As you've followed the last four shortcuts, you're getting closer to being ready to manifest your soulmate. Next comes establishing polarity. Polarity, or opposing energies, creates a magnetic pull in the universe. In the case of romantic relationships, masculine and feminine energy polarize and attract one another. Just like when magnets come together, these energies come together, and they stick. It takes some force to pull them apart. Please be clear that masculine and feminine express as unique energies within every human being, with one energy typically being predominant. They are not the same as gender, nor are they related to our sexual orientation.

Masculine energy is focused, directed, erect, penetrating, assertive, results-oriented, while feminine energy is soft, flowing, creative, receptive, surrendered and expressive.

To create the necessary polarity, the spark, the chemistry, you desire, I always recommend identifying your authentic energetic expressions, called your sexual essence. This will tell you if your essence is predominantly masculine or feminine. Often men and women are shocked to realize the truth about themselves. It frequently explains why love has faded or chemistry has fizzled in the past. Once you know your sexual essence, you'll increase your attractive energy if you align yourself with your authentic masculine or feminine.

United, the masculine and feminine have hot kisses, conversation and lovemaking!

Shortcut #6: Create a Soul Love Vision

As we explore the final steps to ecstatic soulmate attraction, it's important to realize that mixed messages mean mixed results. In other words, you can't successfully manifest your soulmate, if you don't know very clearly what you want to experience with your soulmate.

Notice that I didn't say make a list of all the qualities you want your soulmate to have. A list of qualities will not create the magnetic energy necessary to call in your soulmate. The Law of Attraction requires energy and emotion.

The best way to connect with the energy and emotion is to create your Soul Love Relationship Vision where you describe all of the experiences you want to share with your soulmate and how they make you feel. I suggest writing down all the emotions you will feel in your body when the two of you share these experiences together. When you focus on the experiences and the associated emotions, you'll generate major manifesting power to call in your soulmate!

Shortcut #7: Express Your Desire

For the final shortcut on the path to manifesting your soulmate, it's important to understand the difference between a want and a desire.

Simply put, "want" focuses on the lack of something, wh desire focuses on the presence of something. Want re while desire attracts.

Let me show you what I mean. Here's what "v like when a woman wants to find her soulr a man in my life. I want to wake up with somebody next to me. I want to feel kisses on my neck. I want to be held. When is it ever going to be my turn to find love?" Reading that, can you feel its energy?

Here's what desire looks like when a woman desires her soulmate. The key to success is that when you express the desire, you fully feel the pleasure of the experience in your body, "It feels so good to wake up with a man next to me... and feel his breath on my neck... feel his kisses running down my shoulder... feel his legs wrapped around mine. It feels so good knowing I am so loved. Mmmmmm..."

That's desire, that's feeling it. She is having the experience in the moment she describes it. In contrast, the want example expressed lack, emptiness, and missing-ness.

Unfortunately (or fortunately), you attract more of what you express, so if you're expressing want, and putting all of the "lack" energy into the universe, that's exactly what you're going to get. Specifically, you'll get more lack and you won't attract the man or a woman you're looking for!

However, if you embody and feel the vision you desire, by the Law of Attraction, it has to come to you. Let go of your wants, give up complaining, and own your desire. Feel it every day.

Ecstatic Attraction

After seeing all the shortcuts, you might be thinking, "Oh my gosh, this will take forever." It won't. I promise, it doesn't have to take that long. My clients do all these steps, and more, in as little as 4 months.

Follow the roadmap, take the shortcuts, and if you get stuck along the way, even though you might be tempted to skip over a shortcut, don't. Get help. Get support. Otherwise, you'll keep spinning your wheels, you'll keep detouring instead of taking the fastest path to Soul Love!

About Joanna Shakti

As the founder of Ecstatic Intimacy and the Soul Love Mentor, Joanna Shakti inspires anyone who hungers for deeper love and intimate pleasure to find and build a soulmate partnership where the love runs deep, and the passion stays hot. You might call her a Dating Coach, a Relationship Coach, an Intimacy Coach, a Tantra Teacher or a Spiritual Guide. She's all of that and so much more as she guides men, women, singles and couples to walk the spiritual path of love creating relationships that are an expression of ecstatic authenticity, intimacy and ecstasy. You can learn more about Joanna here: https://ecstaticintimacy.com

REWRITING THE DEFINITION OF SELF-COMPASSION

by Jessica Dugas

"If you want others to be happy, practice compassion.
If you want to be happy, practice compassion."
– Dalai Lama

Dictionary.com says that compassion is the following:

noun
A feeling of deep sympathy and sorrow for another who is stricken by misfortune, accompanied by a strong desire to alleviate the suffering.

I believe this definition is contributing to a lack of compassion for both ourselves and others. By the end of this chapter I hope you'll be able to move forward with a new definition that will allow you to BE compassion each and every moment of your life.

Compassion & People Pleasing

Compassion is both a personal practice and one that is essential to our relationships with others.

Let's start with the easy part: Why is compassion essential to our relationships with others?

In many cases, we find it much easier to show compassion and sympathy toward others than we do for ourselves. How many times have you given someone a break for something they've done when you wouldn't have given yourself the same courtesy? This compassion solely for others can have a tendency to become rampant in one's life if you're not aware of your own intentions and spiritual development.

Have you ever been called a people pleaser? We see this kind of compassion for others before ourselves a lot in people-pleasers. Why? Because it is natural for people-pleasers to put others before themselves. The desire to make others happy tends to come before their own happiness. Therefore, when it comes to compassion, it's the same concept. The desire to be more compassionate to others is more natural than being compassionate to one's self. All of that said, I'm going to twist your thinking again!

I wrote an article not too long ago for *Aspire Magazine* that essentially describes people-pleasing as a superpower! Now, I know your jaw may have hit the floor on that one but hear me out!

Inside my being lives a save-the-world feeling that is SO strong that it's often very difficult for me to hide it. It's an overwhelming sense of compassion. It's more than just wanting to save the world; it's sensing what the world is feeling as if it's all a part of you. My wake-up call came when I was triggered SO badly by someone using that people-pleaser label. I thought to myself, "How can wanting to help others, and seeing other people be happy, be a bad thing?!"

Even in the dictionary, to please means 'to cause to feel happy and satisfied.' I can't, for the life of me, see that as bad.

I believe this is partly where we've gone wrong. As a society, we've, at different times or another, demonized both sides of the coin. Long ago, and even carrying a little into today, people would say it was a bad thing if you were focused too much on yourself. You were called selfish or lazy or even worse if you took time off, took a nap, or did something compassionate toward yourself and put your own personal needs before others. Today, especially in the personal development world, we often see the opposite. As soon as you talk about putting someone or something before yourself, or even being compassionate toward someone to the point where it allows you to reconsider the thoughts and beliefs you once had, it's almost guaranteed that someone will slap a people-pleaser label on you.

Being compassionate toward others is wonderful in many ways. It allows you to see other perspectives helping you to understand others AND yourself better. It makes you happier. It's contagious! If you're showing compassion it encourages others to do the same. It can make you feel good about yourself! The benefits are endless! The one about it making you feel good about yourself, brings me to the more difficult part of compassion, self-compassion.

Self-Compassion is Necessary

If you're currently a person who is not very compassionate toward themselves, I would say go back to the last section and start with being more compassionate toward others. It might seem counter intuitive that compassion toward others CAN be fuel that is needed to ignite a much-needed compassion for yourself.

Self-Compassion is just as necessary to our wellbeing as compassion for others. It's often more difficult to have compassion for ourselves because there are many subconscious beliefs, we have been taught about caring for ourselves and putting ourselves first. Sometimes, our subconscious mind takes it to the next level by tricking us into believing that if we're compassionate toward ourselves, we can't simultaneously have compassion for others. This is probably one of the biggest lies we've allowed ourselves to believe, right up there with not being able to experience a range of emotions all at once.

In general, we are much harder on ourselves today than we might have been years ago. Most of us live in a very fast-paced society where we are constantly encouraged to push, push, push... rise, rise, rise... succeed, succeed, succeed. We see this even in relations between governments and people around the world. If one country is doing better in one area than another, the pressure is on for that country to improve and improve NOW. Now don't get me wrong, competition can be a good thing, but we often aren't getting the full picture which brings me to my next point.

Social media puts all of this in our faces every moment of every day, and it's not always accurate! What we typically see on social media are what I refer to as "light-switch moments". This is where we see someone that was fat and now is thin, someone who was poor and now is rich, or someone who was unsuccessful and now is successful. We are missing all of the 'stuff' in between. We're missing the struggles, the trials, and the failures. We often see this, and it feels SO out of reach for our own lives. We try. Then we may come up against a block of some kind. Then we give up because we feel like we're doing something wrong because it doesn't look as easy as what Sally Influencer posts on Instagram!

The way social media, fast-paced society, and even our leaders encourage us to live isn't contributing to self-compassion. If you feel the pressure, you are not alone! We must learn to be compassionate toward ourselves and get out of comparison mode.

Because we know external forces are not encouraging self-compassion, it is an absolute necessity that we understand that compassion is in our hands! It is 100% on us to decide to be compassionate toward ourselves. No one else is going to do it for us!

So how can we be more compassionate to ourselves in a world that doesn't encourage it? Here are 5 ideas to get you started:

1. Get in the practice of building yourself up often! Congratulate yourself for every single thing you accomplish, no matter how 'small' you think it is. This may not come natural to you but keep up with it and it will become a habit.

2. Forgive yourself EVERY time. No matter what you do that feels like you've failed, offer yourself forgiveness. Also, give yourself the permission TO fail! Failure at some point in your life is inevitable. It's what you choose to do with it that counts!

3. Be present. When you think too far into the past or the future for too long, you forget to be present. Then, when you're not present, you are less likely to have compassion for what you're dealing with in the moment. You are too busy worrying about what has happened or what's to come.

4. Speak to the child in you. Think about it. For those of you who are parents, you'll understand this point. We are often SO much more compassionate toward children than we are adults. We slap a plethora of excuses on this behavior. For example, we might not be compassionate toward an adult because we expect that they should know better. When we picture ourselves as a child, and speak to ourselves in that manner, we will naturally be more compassionate!

5. Create better habits for yourself. Even if you aren't accustomed to speaking to yourself in a compassionate way, you can create habits that are compassionate in nature. They say actions speak louder than words, right? This may be even more powerful than speaking, depending on you as an individual. Choosing to make good choices for yourself is a wonderful act of self-compassion whether you're choosing to eat better, move your

body more, or give up something that may be causing you harm in one way or another.

In addition to these ideas, there are SO many more ways to show self-compassion that it would be impossible to list them all here. What I do know, is that it's up to YOU to find what works for you and implement it! You may not get it right away or you may feel what you're doing isn't working, but it is a practice. This means you need to do something daily, long term, to really see your life change!

Remember, just as having compassion for others fuels self-compassion, self-compassion fuels compassion for the world.

Bonus Thought: If you're struggling to see where you might be already showing yourself compassion in your life, or where you could be more compassionate, ask someone else to give you an outside perspective!

Now, Let's Rewrite That Definition!

Go back to the definition for compassion:

noun
A feeling of deep sympathy and sorrow for another who is stricken by misfortune, accompanied by a strong desire to alleviate the suffering

As I said in the beginning, this definition is part of the reason we have a lack of compassion for ourselves and others. Now that I've shared about the importance of compassion and how easy it can be to choose compassion, I'll explain.

First, compassion is more than just sympathy and sorrow. It's love. It's peace. It's joy. It's frustration. It's SO many emotions. What emotions have you experienced when it comes to compassion?

Next, the definition says, "stricken by misfortune". I have a question for you.

Why are we waiting until we experience misfortune to be compassionate?

Have you ever thought about that before? Honestly, until I sat down to write this chapter, I hadn't given it much thought. However, throughout the writing process, it's a question that has come up for me time and time again.

For me, there is no question that we should show compassion to others all the time, but what if we choose to LIVE self-compassion every moment of every day, in moments of misfortune AND moments of thriving?

The next question is:

What if we acted on that strong desire instead of just having it? What if we put action behind our compassion, especially when it comes to ourselves? Wouldn't compassion be an amazing verb too, not just a noun?

I encourage you to think about these things and I invite you to rewrite the definition of self-compassion with me so that we can thrive in this life, and by extension, change the world:

Self-compassion:

noun
The life-giving feelings you have for yourself every moment of every day, allowing yourself to fully love yourself, forgive yourself, and own your worth, accompanied by a strong desire and actions to change anything that stands in the way of that.

How will you choose to show yourself compassion today, and every day?

About Jessica Dugas

Jessica Dugas is an Intuitive Mentor, International Best Selling Author, and Inspirational Entertainer. She's the creator and host of The Breakthrough Show and the Project Joy Podcast!

She's passionate about helping women empower themselves to live with less stress and more joy, bringing her coaching skills, healing modalities, authentic intuition, holistic lifestyle choices, and spirituality to her Illuminate Your Spirit Community. Outside of her business, Jessica is a wife and homeschooling mom of 6 beautiful children, living a vegan lifestyle. You can learn more about Jessica here: https://www.jessicadugas.com

SELF-LOVE, DATING & MARRIAGE
by Gayla Wick

*"Love yourself first and everything else falls into line.
You really have to love yourself to get
anything done in this world."*
— Lucille Ball

When you read the title of this chapter, did you think, "Oh no, not another person telling me I have to love myself before I can find love?" Did panic creep in knowing you need to treat yourself better, even just a little bit? Perhaps both transpired in the micro flashes of your consciousness. Whatever you thought, you must read on if you want to accelerate finding your love connection. Along the way you just might find yourself feeling happier and healthier – not a bad outcome for anyone.

Magic happens every time a person decides to love themselves. Self-love is a necessity, if we want to be truly happy. Ask any single person struggling to find love and you'll learn that at some level they are hoping someone will come along to provide the love they cannot give themselves. It doesn't have to be this way. In this chapter I'm going to reveal the true secret to attracting and sustaining the love relationship of your dreams.

The first step is to be unshakeable in our commitment to treasure ourselves before looking for love elsewhere. Authentic self-love is the gateway to a healthy love relationship. If that's what you want, then I invite you to consider how you might be falling short in the self-love department or how you might have fallen into the trap of arrogance instead. Needy, self-effacing individuals with low self-esteem are not happy or attractive. Neither are arrogant, demanding ones.

I invite you to consider the role of self-love in dating and marriage. When I talk about self-love, I mean that sense of true worthiness – that feeling in your heart, mind and soul that you are enough. You are worthy of a deep and abiding love relationship and forever commitment. Feeling unworthy is a fertile breeding ground for unhappiness, disease, and abuse of every sort. I know this to be true from my own personal experience and from the clients I've interviewed.

At some point in our lives we all need a wake-up call. Mine came one night as I walked alone on a dark skunk infested dirt road. Deeply unhappy in my marriage, I found myself sobbing, lost and confused. Not knowing how to save myself in the moment, I sat in the middle of the road with my despair. (Not the best idea as I could have been stuck by a car or sprayed by a skunk.) However, it was my dark night of the soul – my wake-up call. The time had come when I could no longer carry on as if nothing was wrong.

If you've ever lost hope, felt despair or had no idea how to go forward then you've experienced your own wake-up call. You may be wondering just what self-love has to do with this situation. It took a long time for me to learn this - the lack of self-love is the root cause of our failure to attract and sustain a healthy love relationship and marriage. No one can love you more than you love yourself. It's not arrogant or selfish to prioritize and care for yourself first and always.

That night I made a critical decision to begin taking care of myself. I realized I'd been feeling like a victim instead of the powerful woman I was! While I did not have a fully thought out plan, I could begin to better care for myself. As they say, I was sick and tired of feeling sick and tired. Being physically and emotionally depleted is not a good place from which to make good decisions. I knew I had to make better choices.

Once I felt stronger, I made the critical decision to save myself from the narcissist I'd married. I'd accepted behavior from him that was unacceptable for far too long in my attempts to make things work out for everyone else. You may have experienced something similar by staying in relationships that diminished your self-worth and happiness. Love, dating and marriage does not need to be this way. There is a path to the soul satisfying love relationship you desire.

At this moment you may not fully understand the real upside to having a healthy dose of self-love. Read on and be honest about how you've been treating yourself. Decide to take action, even if it's just one tiny step. I'll show you how to begin. You'll be happily surprised by the results.

Read this next section with a notebook and pen or highlighter. Underline or highlight anything that resonates with you as something you need to work on. Taking care of yourself first, having self-confidence and valuing yourself is not arrogant – it's essential for living your best life. It's essential for attracting a healthy, loving, supportive intimate partner.

"If you don't love yourself, nobody will. Not only that, you won't be good at loving anyone else. Loving starts with the self."
– Wayne Dyer

Self-Love Plan

Take care of your body. I started by walking every day - outside when the weather was nice and inside on my treadmill when it was cold or rainy. Getting in shape by working out and losing the extra weight I'd been carrying long after the birth of my two children felt empowering. First, I had to be kicked in the butt by a friend. She'd heard me complaining many times about being overweight and told me matter-of-factly, "Why don't you stop talking about it and just do it?" That wasn't the supportive commiseration I was looking for, but it was exactly what I needed! Now, this is me kicking you in the backside to get busy giving yourself a little love.

When someone feels happy and healthy, they attract others who feel likewise. That's the Law of Attraction at work. Like attracts like. Think about the type of life partner and love relationship you desire. Is your partner physically healthy and well-groomed with a warm smile and an air of self-confidence? This type of person will not be attracted to anyone less. Taking care of your body is up to you and will have long-term rewards for your health, vitality and your love attraction story.

If you're in a committed relationship or marriage, physical self-care remains important. You want your partner to take care of themselves and so you must care for yourself as well. Partners who want to keep the romance alive in their intimate relationship know how important this is. Do it first for yourself and then for your relationship.

Body Self-Care:

Eat healthy food, exercise, discard old ratty clothes, invest in good quality clothing and take care of it. Wear clothes that you feel good in, get a new hairstyle if you are unhappy with yours, hire a wardrobe consultant if you need help, get seven to eight hours of sleep, be mindful of your posture, get your teeth cleaned and whitened, and get regular dental and physical check-ups. Try a new activity, enjoy your food and stop obsessing over occasional treats like dessert or a few chips, breathe more deeply and do anything that supports your physical health and brings you joy.

Make your body self-care routine unique for you. The list above is just to stimulate your own ideas. Don't wait until you are ready to date to get started. You must not wait for any reason to begin caring for yourself.

"You have been criticizing yourself for years, and it hasn't worked. Try approving of yourself and see what happens."
– Louise L. Hay

Take care of your mind:

The endless self-critical monkey mind chatter is something we all deal with. You might even be experiencing a ton of that right now, just thinking about your past relationships or even contemplating taking better care of your body. My past negative self-talk kept me stuck in a cycle of misery for far too long.

I discovered that making good decisions could not happen from a chaotic mind. The clarity I was seeking only came when I learned to slow down, breath, and give myself a break from the mind chatter. Just telling myself that I didn't have to make any critical, life altering decisions in that very moment was very helpful. I decided to seek guidance by working with a coach and reading self-help/personal development books. I began a gratitude practice and learned to meditate.

Most importantly, I decided to stop criticizing myself. This is an ongoing work in progress. I encourage you to become more aware of any critical self-talk. It ravages your ability to rise up and become the person you desire to be. As I learned to pivot my negative self-talk to positive affirmations, my life improved. I was making better decisions, taking a stand for myself and my children and refusing to be belittled and mistreated any longer. I developed an increasing capacity to be kinder and gentler with myself. I set new healthy boundaries for any future love relationship.

Everything changes when we are clear about our personal boundaries by loving and caring for our bodies and minds. It becomes easier to walk away from what no longer serves us whether it's bad habits, poor choices, unhealthy relationships or that new potential partner who doesn't seem quite right. Healthy self-love is the best abuse prevention.

When your mind is clear, it's much easier to spot unhealthy, emotionally unavailable individuals. You'll see the players for who they really are and be able to confidently say no thank you to anyone who wants to manipulate or use you as a friend with benefits. From a place of mental clarity, you can reject what doesn't feel right for you. If someone isn't interested, you won't be left wondering what's wrong with you. You'll know it just wasn't the right match.

Being in a committed relationship with the one you love doesn't mean they're perfect. They're perfect for you. They will be irritating sometimes. When that happens, you can stop yourself and remember you have your own quirks and imperfections that just might be annoying to them as well. Mental clarity is the foundation for healthy conflict resolution skills and emotional maturity. You don't need to say everything you think in the moment. Having a healthy mind allows more joy to flow and supports overall healthier life choices.

Mental Health Self-Care:

Take time to clear your mind and rejuvenate. Set your intentions, breathe deeply before speaking, pivot negative self-talk to positive, remember that not all problems have to be solved in the moment, learn to trust yourself, develop your instincts by trusting them more often, and have your own personal interests. Know that bad behavior says more about the person behaving badly, not everything is personal, when you make a mistake quickly forgive yourself and apologize to others when necessary. Try to stop judging others, be open to change, new ideas and other's perspectives and above all let go of old grievances, ideas and ways of being that no longer serve you.

Take care of your heart. As human beings we are hard-wired to be with one another. I believe most singles who profess to be perfectly fine and happy being alone are really trying to convince themselves when instead they desire an intimate partnership. They are fearful of making another love relationship mistake and no longer trust themselves to make good choices.

What has to change? If you're reading this book, then you are still here in spite of any heart breaks you may have experienced. No one wants to have their heart broken but being open to love requires vulnerability. We've all dated the wrong people. Some of us even married someone who didn't turn out to be the one we were going to grow old with. We survived the breakup. There is no possibility of a deep love without the risk of heartbreak. Attracting your authentic love connection requires the vulnerability of an open heart.

Being open to love does not mean allowing just anyone into your life. Be discerning with your choices. Learn to recognize red flags early in a potential relationship and take time to get to know each other. These steps will help you to recognize a relationship that isn't right for you or your future. Not every person who expresses interest in you should be the recipient of your time and attention. You don't need to go out with anyone unless you choose to do so.

Even if you have a date, you can choose not to spend any more time with them unless you want to. Don't be too quick to judge someone as being unsuitable just because you didn't feel a love connection right away. Getting to know someone a little better might be worth it. As you learn to trust your instincts, you'll be less afraid to give love a chance. You may end up with a new friend, even if it isn't a romantic connection. If you experience any red flags with or about this person you can walk away without having invested your time and energy on someone unworthy of you. I know it's hard to do, but just walk away – it's better than hoping they will change.

Heart Self-Care:

Being clear with yourself about what you want and need in a love relationship and being knowledgeable about your deal breakers is protecting your heart in a healthy way. Make a list of values you're looking for in a mate. I use a simple formula for making this list and keeping it short with the most important points. Here's an example:

Physical Attributes:
- Healthy – takes care of himself
- Likes to travel & try new things
- Shares some of my interests
- Generous lover
- Emotional Attributes:
- Loves to cuddle and hold hands
- Open-minded and willing to change his opinions
- Slow to anger
- Emotionally mature
- Intellectual Attributes:
- Educated and articulate
- Likes to learn new things
- Likes to read and discuss a variety of topics
- Takes care of his financial life
- Spiritual Attributes:
- Believes in a higher power
- Supports efforts to protect our planet
- Willing to share and discuss beliefs
- Supports charitable giving

These are a few ideas to help you get started. Keep it positive. Don't include negative attributes. For example, most of us do not want to be in a love relationship with an addict whether it's substance abuse, alcoholism or smoking. By putting 'healthy' and 'takes care of himself' on the list that issue is covered.

One woman told me she did not want to date any more broke losers. She'd been dating guys who couldn't afford to take her out which left her paying for everything. Her list said she was attracting a man who was financially sound and had plans for his future. Great idea!

It's been my experience that people want to know what your boundaries are - for several reasons. First, it gives them clarity about what to expect from you. They like that. Second, when you establish clear healthy boundaries early in a relationship, the other person knows you are a person of high value and standards. This is attractive for the type of mate you're seeking. Third, when you have healthy boundaries you won't tolerate bad behavior from the get-go. This protects your heart, mind and body. You won't be tempted to become involved with someone unworthy of you.

When people in love choose to be with one another in a long-term committed relationship or marriage, hearts are open and vulnerable. A deep and abiding trust is present based upon experience, shared values and healthy boundaries. You must be willing to love yourself enough to establish these rules. Giving your heart to your mate does not mean he or she gets to mistreat you. You must treasure each other and commit to honesty, integrity and full disclosure of needs, wants, desires with shared values and boundaries.

I hope this chapter has inspired you to be more intentional about caring for your body, mind and heart. We can say we love ourselves, but these are mere words until demonstrated through self-care. Once I embraced body, mind and heart self-care, my life began to change dramatically. I met and married the love of my life – a healthy, supportive, loving man that was more than I ever dreamed possible.

Loving yourself sets you up to attract your special someone. Just be mindful not to go crazy spending all your time, energy or money on self-improvements. They are not going to fall in love with your hair or your perfect outfit. They will fall in love with your warm smile, your approachable attitude, your willingness to laugh and have fun even with yourself. Attracting the love of your life and sustaining that delicious relationship requires vulnerability, knowing and respecting your self-worth.

We all have choices in life. We can choose to love, honor and respect our bodies, minds and hearts now. It doesn't matter what our less than optimal choices were in the past. There's no time like the present to choose differently. Take baby steps. You might want to start with a list of things you know you'd like to do. Check it often and reward yourself for progress regardless of how small. Make self-care a priority and make sure your new love or partner takes care of themselves too. Loving and caring for yourself first really is a dating and happy marriage game changer!

About Gayla Wick

Gayla Wick, Denver Love Coach, author, and speaker is the creator of the highly acclaimed "It's All About You" Love Coaching Program for single women. Once a true love skeptic, Gayla shows those who've been disappointed in love how to move past pain and struggle to attract an authentic love relationship. She's the author of The Art of Attracting Authentic Love (A transformational Four-Step Process). Information about her coaching services, book, videos and blog can be found at www.GaylaWick.com.

Made in the USA
Columbia, SC
23 October 2020

23378537R00076